Where Willoughby wintered, 1553

a Zemlya

White Sea

Chancellor met messengers from Russian Czar, 1553

Kola Peninsula

FINLAND

North Cape
Tromso

SWEDEN

Oslo

Where the Italia came down, 1928

DENMARK

Bear I.

NETHERLANDS

SPITSBERGEN

NORWAY

Jan Mayen I.

Shetland Is.

Orkney Is.

ENGLAND

SCOTLAND

Faeroe Is.

Hebrides

IRELAND

ICELAND

Greenland Icecap

sterbygd

GREENLAND

Davis Strait

Osterbygd

THE ARCTIC

Frobisher Bay
Resolution I.

Strait

ROUTES OF EXPLORATION	
BERING 1725-29	
NORDENSKIÖLD 1878-79	
AMUNDSEN 1903-06	
PEARY 1908-09	
BYRD 1926	
THE NAUTILUS 1958	

CANADA

ATLANTIC OCEAN

scale of miles (in radial direction)
0   100   200   400   600

There are six new HORIZON CARAVEL BOOKS
published each year. The titles now available are:

HEROES OF POLAR EXPLORATION
KNIGHTS OF THE CRUSADES

EX LIBRIS

STEPHEN FRIEDLANDER

COVER: *Robert E. Peary, who once conquered the Arctic, is still the ideal polar hero.*
PORTRAIT BY JOHN JOHANSEN, COLLECTION OF KANE LODGE NO. 454 F. & A.M.

FRONT END SHEET: *An explorers' map of the Arctic shows the historic routes to the Pole.*

TITLE PAGE: *A midnight sun shines as a beacon to polar explorers in this ancient woodcut.*
N.Y. PUBLIC LIBRARY, RARE BOOK DIVISION

BACK END SHEET: *The brief, dramatic story of Antarctica is outlined in this colorful map.*

A
HORIZON
CARAVEL
BOOK

HEROES OF POLAR
EXPLORATION

By the Editors of
HORIZON MAGAZINE
Author
RALPH K. ANDRIST
In consultation with
REAR ADMIRAL GEORGE J. DUFEK, U.S.N. (RET.)
Director, The Mariners Museum, Newport News, Virginia

Published by
AMERICAN HERITAGE PUBLISHING CO., INC.

Book trade distribution by Meredith Press
Institutional distribution by Harper & Brothers

FIRST EDITION
Library of Congress Catalogue Card Number: 62-16256
© 1962 by American Heritage Publishing Co., Inc., 551 Fifth Avenue, New York 17,
New York. All rights reserved under Berne and Pan-American Copyright Conventions.

FOREWORD

I saw the great white Antarctic ice pack for the first time in 1939 from the bridge of the old wooden icebreaker the U.S.S. *Bear*. The *Bear* was the flagship of Admiral Richard E. Byrd, and I was a lieutenant and the ship's navigator. We were sailing eastward, just north of the pack, en route from Little America to the Palmer Peninsula. There we planned to build another permanent installation, East Base, from which to conduct further exploration.

Admiral Byrd, a bluff, handsome man, turned to speak to me. He asked what I thought of the beautiful but desolate scene. My reply, which was quite factual, failed to satisfy him. He told me then of his love for that frozen, mysterious land and of his faith that some day it would unlock its mysteries and provide rich returns—if not in material wealth or strategic value, at least in scientific knowledge.

That faith, in various forms, is what has kept polar explorers going to the ends of the earth. As for myself, when we returned to the United States, I vowed I had seen my last of the polar regions. But I underestimated the force of the lure that draws men back to the poles. Since then I have made two expeditions to the Arctic and five more to the Antarctic.

This book tells the stories of men who sought and conquered the poles in the great era of exploration which lasted from about 1750 to the first years of this century. These are tales of remarkable achievement, sacrifice, and heroism; and also of failure, starvation, and tragedy.

Since the passing of that great age, the methods of polar exploration have changed considerably: the fragile wooden ships and the skittish dog teams have been replaced by icebreakers, tractors, and aircraft. But the snow-covered landscape remains the same—fantastic, challenging, forbidding —demanding the very best that men and nations have to offer.

GEORGE J. DUFEK

Men and machines now probe the polar regions with an ease and efficiency never before dreamed possible. Falling into crevasses was once a fatal mishap for explorers. But in modern times, even a vehicle as heavy as a Sno-cat (left) can be maneuvered out with low-geared treads and metal ramps.

A North American Eskimo, armed with a spear and a bow and arrow, is on guard to welcome a British ship to the frozen North in this watercolor painted in 1832.

CONTENTS

I AT THE ENDS OF THE EARTH

Eric the Red was an adventurer, a swaggering Viking. Like his father, he had a quick, dangerous temper. His father had been forced to leave Norway and flee to Iceland because he had killed a man in a fight. Now Eric, in turn, was fighting and brawling and had already killed two opponents. The parliament of Iceland therefore decreed that he and his followers should be banished for three years.

Thus, in A.D. 982, Eric the Red prepared for a voyage that still stands as a high point in the history of polar exploration. He set sail from Iceland and discovered Greenland, that vast, ice-capped island that comes nearer the North Pole than any other land.

Eric and his companions had grown up in Iceland. Their Viking forebears had journeyed to Iceland not for adventure but to escape from Europe's warring kings and crowded valleys. They had loaded their cattle and household goods into the longboats and sailed confidently over the stormy seas that until then had kept any other Europeans from claiming possession of that distant island. In fact, only two groups of voyagers are known to have reached Iceland before the Vikings. One was led by Pytheas, a Greek scientist-adventurer of the fourth century B.C. He had journeyed north and west to England in search of tin, and somehow he had continued even farther north. The other group was a band of Irish monks who drove their coracles—small boats made of hides stretched over crude wooden frames—into Arctic waters in A.D. 825 seeking refuge from the wars of the Dark Ages.

But, after the arrival of the first Vikings, Iceland rapidly became overpopulated with immigrants. And if Eric had not been forced to become an explorer because of his

Across Antarctica's wild emptiness (left) trudge the men of one of the expeditions that tried to reach the South Pole—Robert F. Scott's fateful attempt of 1911. At right is a bust of Pytheas, the Greek explorer who sailed north to Iceland in 325 B.C. and became history's first polar hero.

11

Memorial stones, intricately carved and colorfully painted, helped preserve the Vikings' traditions and myths. At right is a Viking tombstone with the longboat emblem that was the mark of nobility. Carved into the stone are scenes that dramatize a dead Viking's heroic end on the field of battle. The photograph below shows the desolate landscape that greeted Viking settlers when they sailed into the Greenland fjords.

banishment, others surely would have gone out to look for new pastures beyond the horizon. For there were rumors of an uninhabited land to the west, stories of a bleak coastline sighted by Gunnbjörn Ulfsson about 900.

It was that coast that Eric determined to explore. After weeks of sailing, he eventually found the western land, its craggy promontories disappearing into the mists of the North. He then explored its southeastern and southwestern shores, discovering the former to be cold and forbidding, the latter lush and promising. At the end of his three years' banishment he returned home to sing the praises of the new land which he, in hopes of making it sound attractive, called Greenland. The Vikings of Iceland listened, and during the next year made ready to follow him.

As a result of Eric's discovery and his leadership, a fleet of twenty-five ships carrying colonists and livestock went back with him to Greenland in 986. The settlers did not know, of course, what dangers lay in Greenland or what massive shifts of climate can occur in the Arctic, where the whole character of an area may change in a season. Yet by following their explorer-hero, they were exposing themselves and their descendants to a tragic fate. Like other followers of future explorers, the Greenland colonists would find that the polar regions are hostile to man.

Eric had searched carefully for the best possible location for his settlement and had selected a site on the west coast, near the southern tip of the island. It was not farmland, but the Norsemen were cattle raisers, not plowmen, and the grass grew thick and high in the pastures during the short Greenland summers.

The settlement thrived as more colonists came. When every portion of usable land had a farm on it, another settlement was begun about two hundred miles up the coast. *Osterbygd* (Eastern Settlement) was the name given to the first region settled; the second one was called *Vesterbygd* (Western Settlement). Eventually, Christianity came to Greenland, and the heathen Viking settlers in both colonies became Christian converts.

For the first centuries of its existence Greenland was a republic like Iceland, its parent. Then, in 1261, the Norwegian king convinced the Greenlanders—and the Icelanders a year or so later—that they should submit to his rule. They agreed, and soon afterward the king decreed that only Norwegian ships could trade with Greenland. Even Icelanders were forbidden to trade with their

13

A French map maker, Guillaume Le Testu, drew this World Map and Winds *for an atlas published in 1555. It show.*
a globe that has been cut in two, pulled open, and printed inside and outside. Like most early maps, Le Testu's was base

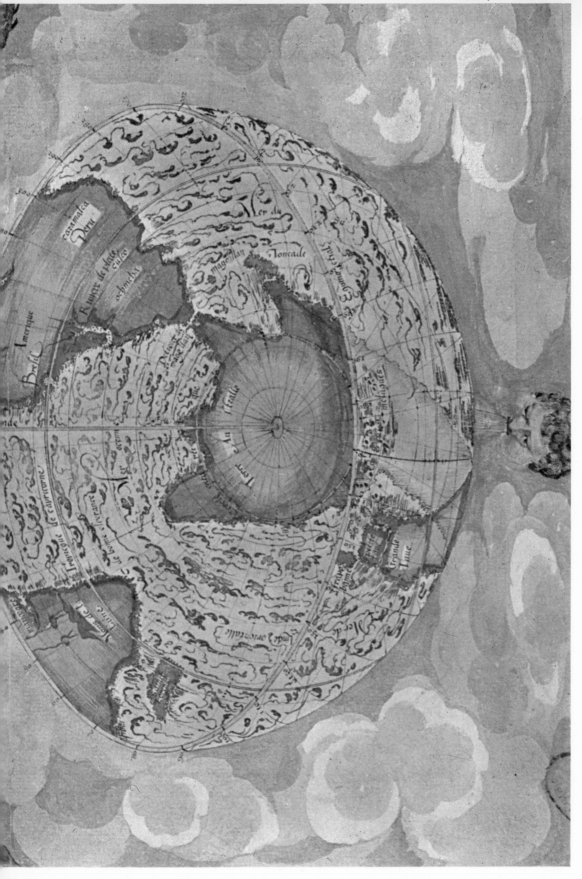

argely on supposition, but his concept of polar geography was amazingly accurate. Arctic regions (left) are seen surround-ng an icy polar sea. Antarctica (above) is a land mass which in places extends as far north as the tip of South America.

neighbor, under penalties that came to include death.

In return, the king promised that Norwegian trading ships would be sent regularly to Greenland, which at that time sustained some three thousand colonists. His assurance must have sounded attractive to his new western subjects, whose commerce with Europe was not always on a definite schedule. But the promise was gradually ignored, and ships bound for Greenland became less and less frequent. Vessels of other nations sometimes violated the Norwegian king's ban, but a curtain was beginning to lower between the Norse settlements and the rest of the world.

There were occasional contacts between the mainland of Europe and the Greenland colonies during the fourteenth century; but then, silence and darkness. Nothing further was seen or heard of those who had followed Eric the Red. In some mysterious manner the settlements had been wiped out, perhaps by Eskimo attacks, perhaps by weather.

And since then, the mystery has been solved only in part. For centuries, even the location of the Greenland colonies was forgotten. Not until 1921, after a lengthy search, were the settlements rediscovered by a team of archeologists. The stone walls of the buildings were the first relics to be found. But a more dramatic discovery was made in the cemeteries: there the dead lay in soil that had been frozen since the days when they were laid to rest.

Dust had not returned to dust in the eternal cold of the graveyards. The dead Vikings slept holding their crosses in folded hands; their clothing of shaggy woolen lay in the same creases as on the day of burial. Their well-preserved bodies were gnomelike, undersized, with bones bent from rickets and other deficiency diseases.

Examination of these bodies revealed that few of the Vikings had lived beyond their early twenties. Undernourished after many years of insufficient food, Greenland's once-vigorous settlers had become stunted dwarfs. One explanation for this is that as Greenland's trade with Europe was beginning to slacken, her climate coincidentally was undergoing a change. Gradually the cold became more and more severe. Pastures no longer grew tall grass, and the thinning herds of cattle soon could not supply all the food the settlements needed. A slow process of malnutrition finally destroyed an entire civilization.

Only now, in modern times, have men begun to acquire sufficient knowledge to live and travel in the Arctic and

Ancestors of these Eskimos, who
were brought to Norway in 1564,
often quarreled with the settlers
in Greenland and may have helped
destroy the Viking colonies there.

Their prows carved to look like dragons' heads,
the Viking longboats resembled unfriendly sea
monsters as they sliced through the waves. Viking sailors believed their ships' forbidding
appearance would frighten away evil spirits and
ward off potential enemies. The ship above was
painted in 1922 by John Taylor Arms. At left
above, topped by a conical helmet, is an ancient
Swedish Viking head carved from bone. Below the
head is a wooden cross that was found in a Norse-
man's grave on Greenland four centuries after
the Viking settlements were last heard from.
The inscription reads, "Jesus Christ, help me."

Antarctic without tragedy as their constant companion. After centuries of polar exploration, the mysteries lying at the ends of the earth are gradually being solved.

One of the most challenging of them has been the difference between the North and the South poles—a difference that has affected techniques of exploration. Indeed, it is now understood that about the only similarity between the north and south polar regions is the predominant whiteness of their winters. Although both regions are incredibly cold, Antarctica is the colder because it is mostly a high ice-plateau with no supply of heat such as exists under the thin ice pack covering the circulating waters of the Arctic Ocean. The Antarctic, in fact, averages 10 degrees colder than the Arctic.

In summer, at the North Pole, the temperature stays near the freezing point as the pack ice melts. At the South Pole, even on the warmest summer days, the temperature remains well below freezing.

The two regions differ in terms of topography and physical environment as well as of weather. According to the Antarctic explorer Rear Admiral George J. Dufek, "It is as if a mythical force [had] thrust its thumb down on the North Pole and a bulge appeared at the South Pole." For the North Pole is near the center of the Arctic Ocean, which is ten thousand feet deep. This body of water, choked with ice, is surrounded by the northern portions of Canada, Alaska, Scotland, the coasts of Labrador and Europe, and

Icebergs, ice floes, and freezing temperatures greeted explorers at both ends of the earth. At left are men of one of Captain Cook's expeditions inspecting icebergs in Antarctic waters. At right are the Irish monks who sailed north to look for new lands in A.D. 825.

such polar islands as Greenland, Iceland, and Spitsbergen.

The South Pole lies near the center of the great land-mass of Antarctica—at a spot ten thousand feet above sea level. About 90 per cent of the world's ice is in Antarctica, covering the continent like a frozen dome. The average altitude of this frosted land is six thousand feet, with peaks that rise as high as twelve and fifteen thousand feet. In some places the accumulated ice itself is nearly two miles thick. Thus Antarctica has the greatest expanse of high tableland in the world—greater than the lofty Andes of South America and comparable only to the plateau country of Tibet.

The Arctic supports a human population of more than a million—which subsists on the land along with polar bears, reindeer, seals, caribou, and a great variety of birds. But Antarctica is like a cold desert, lacking the pine forests that grow in parts of the Arctic, lacking even so much as a shrub. Unlike the Arctic, the interior of Antarctica is virtually lifeless—the only major land mass on earth that does not support a native human population. What animals there are—penguins, albatrosses, and some species of petrel—live off the fish in the water at the continent's outer rim. Or, as in the case of the skua gull, they may live by preying on their fellow creatures.

With more than five million square miles, Antarctica is larger in area than the United States and Mexico combined. Less than a hundred square miles of this land is naked earth, free from a permanent blanket of ice. And, for six hundred miles surrounding the continent, ice fills the turbulent seas. In winter the bays and coastal waters are frozen solid. Only in the short summer period, from December through March, when violent storms and tides break up the ice pack, can ships reach or leave the continent.

Exploration in the North is older by several centuries than it is in the South, for the Arctic was never so remote. The early Vikings were attracted to it, before the tragic end of the Greenland colonies, as naturally as Italians like Columbus were drawn to the sun-warmed seas that bordered their land. And from that attraction gradually developed the dream that the very top of the world might be reached.

The polar dreams that stirred the imagination of the world a hundred years ago and more have been largely forgotten now that both poles have been conquered. But the heroic deeds of the great explorers will always be remembered. They remain among the proudest memories shared by men.

*Equipment for a scientific research station in Antarctica is unloaded from
a Coast Guard icebreaker anchored near Cape Hallett. Modern technology
has helped tame the elements, but polar geography is as formidable as ever.*

21

II ARCTIC ROUTES TO RICHES

After the haunting episode of the Greenland Vikings, several hundred years passed before men would turn their attention to the Arctic once again. And, when they did, they were not motivated by the desire to colonize or the urge to explore—at least not for the mere sake of exploration. Men returned to the Arctic in the hope of achieving wealth through trade; they were seeking a sea route to the Orient.

The first English expedition sent out for this purpose sailed in 1553, heading in a northeasterly direction. The fleet of three ships, which had been purchased and outfitted by an association of merchants, was commanded by Sir Hugh Willoughby. The ships proceeded as far as North Cape, the very northern tip of Norway, beyond the Arctic Circle. Then a sudden and violent storm caused one vessel to become separated from the others.

The captain of the single vessel, Richard Chancellor, sailed his ship down into the White Sea, where messengers brought him an invitation to visit the czar in Moscow. The result of their meeting led, in 1555, to the establishment of the Muscovy Company, which for twenty years provided an immensely profitable exchange of trade between Russia and England. (See map at front of book.)

Commander Willoughby was not so fortunate as Chancellor. With the two ships that remained in his command he cruised off northern Russia, seeing no signs of human life. When winter approached he took his vessels into a good harbor on the Kola Peninsula, and there he tried to bring his men through the long period of darkness. Fishermen found them the next summer, all dead, most likely from scurvy, that vitamin-deficiency disease that was the curse of polar explorers even into the twentieth century. A diary left by Willoughby told of the long wait

Arctic waters were once thought to be alive with ship-gobbling monsters like the one in the sixteenth-century woodcut at left. The picture below, from a fourteenth-century manuscript, shows early voyagers to the East navigating by stars.

The riches of Cathay, reported by Marco Polo after his voyage of 1295, spurred explorers on to find new eastward routes. Europeans saw their dreams of luxury come to life in art such as this Indian tapestry. It shows a group of Dutch merchants amid the elegance and splendor of an oriental court.

for the help that never came and of their hopeless courage.

In 1576 England turned to the search for a north-*west* passage. The shift in direction was due mainly to the persistence of one man, Martin Frobisher. Frobisher argued and pleaded with an indifferent England for ten years until he found backers to finance an expedition. They fitted him out with a fleet of just three vessels—the *Gabriel* and the *Michael* and a smaller ship called a pinnace.

The fleet left England on June 7, 1576. On July 8 the pinnace with her four-man crew was lost in a storm. And, after passing Greenland, the crew of the *Michael* became so unnerved by the constant presence of huge drifting icebergs that they turned their ship around and headed for home.

Only the *Gabriel* was left now, with Frobisher aboard. This fearless explorer, who had lived at sea since his early teens, was not about to turn back. He pressed onward until he had made a landfall on Resolution Island—off the southern tip of what is now known as Baffin Island. Then he sailed into a waterway that he assumed would lead him eventually to Asia. He was certain that this waterway, which later turned out to be a bay (Frobisher Bay), was indeed the northwest passage he had been seeking. And he assumed that the Eskimos who rowed out to meet him in their skin-covered canoes were actually Asians.

He hauled one of the natives aboard the *Gabriel* so he could prove his triumph at home.

Frobisher had intended to remain in the Arctic and explore the northwest passage he thought he had discovered. Five of his men disappeared, however, leaving him shorthanded and forcing him to return home early. The Eskimo he brought with him was unable to adjust to the change in climate; he caught cold and died soon after he arrived in England.

In addition to the doomed Eskimo, Frobisher's first expedition yielded a piece of heavy black rock. An assayer, assumed to be an expert in analyzing ores and minerals, said there was gold in the rock. As a result, Frobisher had no trouble getting money to back his second voyage. He set out the next year with three ships, hoping to find the spot where the black rock had come from and see if there was a plentiful supply.

The expedition was successful on both counts. The ships returned heavily laden with ore that won a glowing report from the assayer. Now all England was eager to pour funds into the Frobisher enterprise. Even Queen Elizabeth and her court invested money. Elizabeth's goal was wealth for her kingdom, and in this respect Frobisher's enterprise seemed a shrewd investment. The Queen had believed that if Arctic exploration could provide a route to riches it was a worthwhile gamble. And now that the region promised to yield riches of its own, the gamble seemed far less risky. Thus in 1578, when Frobisher began his third expedition, he had no less than fifteen ships. His mission: to bring back great quantities of the gold-filled black rock.

When the fleet returned, the blow fell for Frobisher. Another assayer—apparently an honest one this time—disclosed that the black rock actually contained only worthless iron pyrite ("fool's gold"). Frobisher was disgraced, and his claim to having found a northwest passage and to having reached the very frontiers of Cathay was discredited. He redeemed himself later, however, by serving successfully in the navy when Spain's great Armada sailed against England.

John Davis, who followed Frobisher to the North, was a completely different type of Elizabethan—quiet instead of flamboyant, a careful planner and observer, and the most accomplished scientific seaman of his time. Beginning in 1585 he made three voyages from England up the west coast of Greenland. On his last voyage, in 1587, he reached latitude 72°41' north, in what is now called Baffin Bay.

A Flemish artist, visiting London, drew his impression of the Eskimo that Martin Frobisher brought back to England from the Arctic in 1576.

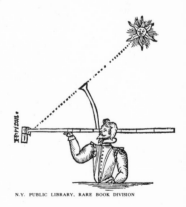

This device, used to determine latitude, was called the 45° Back Staff. It was developed by John Davis, one of the foremost navigators of the sixteenth century.

25

MARTIN FROBISER MILES
GVALTERI CHARLETONI M.D.

26

Davis contributed more to the knowledge of the Arctic than anyone before him. In addition to his geographical discoveries, he wrote about the Eskimos, about the plants that grew in Greenland, and about the icebergs and ice floes—sheets of floating ice—that drifted through the channels. His reports were of great value to other explorers because of his expressed optimism that a northwest passage did exist and could be found. In 1588, however, England's exploration of the Arctic came to a halt as the conflict with Spain grew into a full-scale war and all of England's ships were needed to guard her vulnerable seacoast. By this time the Dutch had seized leadership of the search for a northern route to Cathay.

The Dutch had always been England's rivals in the struggle for naval and commercial leadership. Since 1555, when England established the Muscovy Company, Dutch merchants had looked with envy at the riches flowing into London from Eastern lands. They were now eager to find a passage through the Arctic—preferably an eastern passage, one that would enable them also to share in the rich trade with Russia.

The greatest of the early searchers for the northeast passage was indeed a Dutchman, Willem Barents. He made his first voyage into the waters north of Russia in 1594 as chief pilot of a four-ship expedition that had been sent to find a passage to Cathay. He might well have succeeded, for the Kara Sea was free of ice that year. But, instead of pushing on, Barents returned home to report the progress he had made. The next year he set out with seven ships. But the ice was back in the Kara Sea, making it impassable, and the expedition was a failure.

In 1596 the merchants of Holland felt that they were able to send out only two ships to look for a northern route to the East. Barents piloted one of them. Instead of striking out toward the East after clearing North Cape, the ships continued northward. Their course soon brought them among the ice floes and then to an uncharted island which still carries the name the Dutch seamen gave it— Bear Island—following a battle with a lean and hungry polar bear.

At left is a portrait of Martin Frobisher, the man who started England's search for a northwest passage. At right are relics of the 1596 expedition of the Dutch explorer Willem Barents—a decorative pitcher, an instrument of navigation, and a wooden compass card. These articles were found after 274 years in what remained of Barents' makeshift winter cabin.

27

One member of the Barents expedition shoots at a polar bear while the others chop through the ice. Barents' abandon

...ip is in the background of this picture, which was published in 1598 along with an official account of the voyage.

Farther north they made another discovery: the craggy, desolate islands which they named Spitsbergen, meaning "pointed mountains." In the seas around the islands, seals, whales, and walrus lived and raised their families. These animals added up to a maritime wealth that was soon to provoke open conflict between the English and the Dutch.

The ships of the Barents expedition were finally halted by ice at about latitude 80° north—six hundred nautical miles from the Pole. This was the northernmost point reached by Europeans up to this time. Soon afterward, the captains of the two ships disagreed about the course to be followed, and Barents' ship headed eastward. It entered the Kara Sea and was stopped by pack ice just off the northeast coast of Novaya Zemlya.

Instead of retreating at once, Barents hesitated, and the ice floes closed in and trapped his ship, making her timbers groan and shriek from the enormous pressure. It was obvious to Barents and his men that they would have to spend the winter in this forbidding place. If they survived, they would become the first Europeans ever to winter above the Arctic Circle.

The men moved ashore to a site they called Ice Haven. There they built a house of local driftwood and timbers from the ship. The roof was made of sails held down by the weight of sand. Bunks were built along one wall, and heat was supplied by the ship's stove. There were books to read and a Dutch clock to tick away the hours as the long winter progressed.

Gerrit de Veer, a young barber-surgeon in the company, did his best to bring the men through the experience in good health and high spirits. He had a tub constructed from a large wine cask and made the men take warm baths every week. He insisted that they exercise as much as possible, and he arranged entertainment to keep up their morale. But, as there was little he could do about their diet, the expedition lost five of its seventeen men, probably from scurvy.

In mid-June, when his ship was still icebound, Barents decided that the only way out of Ice Haven was to make an open-boat voyage to the Kola Peninsula, sixteen hundred miles away. The explorers set out, taking to the water when possible, hauling their two small boats over the ice fields when necessary. Although the boats leaked considerably, the men were afraid to pause on land to rest or make repairs because of the presence of polar bears, which were generally hostile.

The compass at left, made in England in 1750, is an ornate version of the simple instrument that was used by seamen in Willem Barents' time and even as early as Columbus. Below is the interior of the cabin that Barents and his men built at Ice Haven on the northeast tip of Novaya Zemlya. They used scrap wood from their ship to make bunk beds and converted a wine cask into the bathtub seen at right.

31

Barents himself did not complete the voyage. He had been weak and ailing for a long time, and he died of cold and exposure soon after the difficult return trip began. But three months later his men arrived at the Kola Peninsula, where, by chance, they were found by the other ship of the expedition. After parting company with the vessel Barents commanded, this one had wintered very comfortably on the White Sea.

For the next 274 years no human being came anywhere near the lonely site of Ice Haven. Then, in 1871, some Norwegian seal hunters stopped there and found remains of the house that Barents and his men had built. It had been knocked about by generations of polar bears, but its framework stood, and the frigid air had kept decay to a minimum. De Veer's bathtub was still there, as were other relics including the old Dutch clock. And found at last was Barents' account of the voyage. He had placed it in a

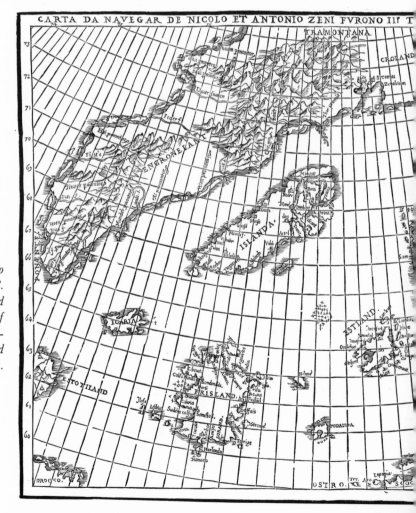

This map, drawn in 1390 by Nicolo Zeno, was not printed until 1558. It inaccurately showed Greenland joined to Norway. And because of this error, it helped persuade explorers that they could never find a northeasterly route to the Orient.

powder horn so there would be a record of the expedition, even if everyone perished.

By 1597, the year Barents and his men set out from Ice Haven, Holland had ceased to be interested in the dangerous business of sending out northern expeditions. But the English, who continued to hope that a profitable route to the East could be found, redoubled their efforts.

In the interest of England's Muscovy Company, Henry Hudson was sent out in 1607. His charter was to reach Cathay, if he could, by sailing directly over the North Pole. This notion did not seem so improbable then as it does now, because for hundreds of years people believed that the central basin of the Arctic Ocean remained unfrozen inside pack ice through which ships could pass.

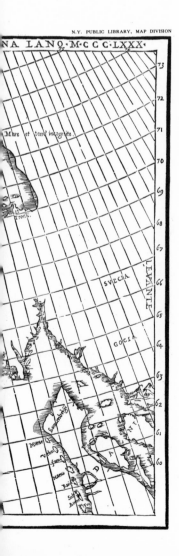

Hudson's was the first known attempt to reach the North Pole. He was not successful, but he did get as far north as latitude 80°23'. This was roughly 575 nautical miles from the Pole, a record that would stand for 166 years. Hudson rediscovered Spitsbergen and confirmed Barents' reports of the rich catches of whales and seals in its waters. He also found a cold, rocky island that he named Hudson's Tutches. It is now called Jan Mayen Island.

Hudson set out again in 1608. This time he hoped to find a northeast passage and would not attempt to reach the North Pole. Like those who had sailed before him, however, he was met by heaped-up pack ice in the Vaigach and Kara straits. Hudson was in favor of pushing onward, but his men rallied against him; the mutiny, not the ice, forced him to turn back.

After a voyage of exploration to the North American continent, Hudson was back in the Arctic in 1610. This time his English backers hoped he would find a north*west* passage. His ship was the *Discovery*, and she was jinxed even before she had left port. Her second-in-command, Robert Juet, was the man who had led the mutiny against Hudson two years earlier. Long before the *Discovery* reached Iceland, it was apparent that Juet had not changed. The seas were serene and smooth, but Juet was sullen, whispering darkly of mutiny and murder.

Entering Hudson Strait was perilous for the *Discovery* because of the ice floes that ground through the channel. But once beyond these treacherous waters, Hudson was able to explore the eastern shore of what became known as Hudson Bay. Then he moved southward into James Bay, where, with cold weather approaching, he wintered.

His men survived the winter in better condition than

33

was usual in a day when scurvy was the common and often fatal occupational disease of Arctic explorers. But, as the men had little with which to occupy their thoughts during the long period of idleness, they became vulnerable to the talk of mutiny that was spread by Juet and his band of malcontents.

It was well past the middle of June when the *Discovery* was free from her ice bonds. By then Hudson had lost control of his crew, and the mutineers had taken over. Hudson, his young son, and five crew members who had been loyal to their captain were put into the ship's boat and dropped behind. They were never seen or heard from again.

Four of the leading mutineers were later killed while attempting to trade with the Eskimos, and Robert Juet died during the trip back to England. Robert Bylot, mate of the *Discovery* under Hudson, brought the ship and his fellow survivors home safely, and, surprisingly, all were absolved of their guilt as mutineers. Mutiny at sea was punishable by death, but Hudson's men were the only ones who knew how to navigate the newly discovered northern waters. It would have seemed shortsighted, however just, for these talents to expire at the end of a gallows rope.

Robert Bylot made other voyages in the *Discovery*, exploring the coasts of Hudson Bay and trying to pierce the impenetrable, ice-filled waters of Foxe Basin. On one of these voyages—the most ambitious one he ever made—his pilot was William Baffin. Although Bylot commanded the expedition, Baffin was to receive sole credit for its achievements. A skilled and experienced navigator, Baffin piloted the *Discovery* along the west coast of Greenland until she had passed the farthest point reached by John Davis, 72°41' north. Baffin navigated the ship through the thickening ice floes, picking a way wherever an open path developed.

Baffin and Bylot traversed the length of the great body of water now known as Baffin Bay and sailed into its narrow northward extension, which they named Smith Sound after one of their patrons, Sir Thomas Smith. At about 75°45' north the ice finally stopped them and they turned back, sailing down the west side of Baffin Bay. They passed two broad channels which they named Jones Sound and Lancaster Sound after two other patrons.

The scope of their accomplishments was startling. Smith Sound was the path through which the North Pole one day would be reached. Lancaster Sound was to be the great avenue for seeking the northwest passage. It would be 236 years before any other men would get so far

Whaling ships of many nations sailed to the Arctic in the seventeenth and eighteenth centuries. Most of the whalers came from Holland and England, countries that profited greatly from discoveries made by early explorers.

Sir Thomas Smith, a rich merchant-adventurer, was the guiding force behind many seekers of the northwest passage. He helped support the fateful voyage that ended with the death of Henry Hudson in 1610.

north in those same areas. It would be 202 years before anyone would even verify the existence of Baffin Bay.

The Baffin-Bylot expedition, which was the last voyage of the durable *Discovery*, marked the high point of the prolonged search for a northwest passage. Subsequent expeditions were limited to poking around the increasingly familiar waters of Hudson Bay. The chronicles of these voyages were, more often than not, tales of hardship and suffering. None provides a grimmer example of what men underwent to explore the North than the story of Jens Munk.

At 41, Munk had been a whaler, a merchant captain, a fighter against pirates, and a captain in the Danish navy. He had been picked by Denmark's King Christian IV to lead a Danish expedition in 1619 to seek a passage through Hudson Bay to the Pacific. With two ships and sixty-four men, Munk passed through Hudson Strait so late in the summer that he hardly had time to prepare for winter. He took his ships to the west side of Hudson Bay, and then at the mouth of the Churchill River drew them as close to shore as possible. He built barricades to protect the ships from wind- and tide-driven ice.

The men complained of the bitter cold but remained in reasonably good health for much of the winter. Then, one by one, they began to fall ill. By the end of January they were dying of scurvy. By June only four men were still alive. Two were in a hut on shore, and Munk himself and a sailmaker lay aboard ship in the company of corpses. When the stench of the bodies became overwhelming, Munk summoned all his strength to drag himself on deck. He signaled to the survivors on shore who came out to help their captain across the ice and on to land.

The warm June sun had encouraged a few early sprouts of green to pop up through the earth. Munk and his men dug up everything they could find, sucking the juices out of roots because disease had loosened their teeth and chewing was out of the question.

The survivors dragged the smaller of their two vessels into deeper waters and in mid-July put up sail at last. The sailmaker had died, which meant that only three men of the original sixty-four survived this disastrous expedition.

After Jens Munk there were two more fruitless expeditions, both in 1631, to find a way to reach the Pacific. Then the search for a northwest passage subsided as another period of Arctic exploration came to a close. Explorers and adventurers were quickly replaced by whale hunters sailing in northern waters. From English, French, Dutch, Danish, Norwegian, and Hanseatic ports they came—and fought fiercely for the choicest hunting areas. In whaling, as well as in fur trapping and seal hunting, men found the elusive riches that the North had always seemed to promise.

Whaling had begun in the Arctic soon after Henry Hudson reported seeing the great mammals in the fjords and surrounding waters of Spitsbergen. The whalers wandered far in search of prey, but few reported what discoveries they had made. By maintaining secrecy they hoped to retain the advantage that came with their exclusive knowledge. In some instances the world had to wait many years for explorers to "find" seas and shores that had been known to whaling captains for a long, long time.

For most of the seventeenth and eighteenth centuries the whaling industry flourished in the Arctic, and the northern seas were almost the sole domain of whale hunters and their ships. Explorers were destined to return, however. They would sail northward once again—and when they came, they would fly the flags of many nations.

Jens Munk wrote and published an account of his 1619 voyage to the Arctic. This woodcut, which appeared in the book, shows where Munk and his men spent the winter.

III TRAGEDY IN THE ARCTIC

While Western Europe was enjoying the rich rewards of whaling, Russia moved into the field of exploration. The curiosity of her rulers was stretching toward the uncharted regions beyond her northern borders.

Russia's participation in Arctic exploration had had commercial as well as geographic origins. For many years her pioneers had been moving eastward across Siberia's empty tundra, claiming and colonizing the virgin land in the name of the czar.

By the beginning of the eighteenth century, these overland explorers had reached the Sea of Okhotsk, which flows into the Pacific. Then, in 1725, Czar Peter the Great pushed the expansion program one step further. He set in motion a vast undertaking that he hoped would carry Russian ships over the top of the world. He wanted his ships to be the first to find a waterway linking the Pacific and Arctic oceans. Then, if they did, he would know for certain that the Asian and North American continents were separate and not joined.

Vitus Bering, an enterprising Dane in the service of the Imperial Russian Navy, was assigned to command this project. His task was a formidable one: to take an overland expedition from St. Petersburg in European Russia across five thousand miles of virtually trackless Siberian wilderness to the coastal frontier town of Okhotsk. Then he was to build his ships and proceed by sea to find an Arctic-Pacific waterway.

The long journey across Siberia was made even more difficult by the need to transport supplies and men over the swirling waters of four of Russia's mightiest rivers. Bering's men completed the last leg by hauling the expedition's supplies and equipment on sledges across a frozen

Landing on Kamchatka Peninsula, Bering saw Eskimos like these making fire by twirling sticks on stones. The engraving above, printed in 1793, was rendered from an on-the-spot drawing.

Vitus Bering's last expedition to the Arctic was immensely successful, but it ended with the explorer's death on the beach at Bering Island (at left).

39

Two civilizations meet face to face as men of John Ross's voyage of 1818 try to communicate with the Eskimos on ice-covered Lancaster Sound. Sailing west-

ward through the sound, en route to Bering Strait, Ross imagined he saw mountains in the way, so he turned back, ending his search for a northwest passage.

no-man's-land until Okhotsk was finally reached. Then, in 1729, after many delays, Bering made the long voyage around Kamchatka Peninsula, which he charted for the first time. After that, he headed into the strait that later bore his name.

To his left, as he sailed northward, he could see the easternmost tip of Asia. To his right he could see nothing, for a fog hung low on the horizon, shrouding the Alaska coastline. To prove conclusively that the two continents were not joined somewhere ahead of him, Bering would have had to follow the northern coast of Siberia until he reached landmarks already charted from the west. But the summer was waning. Bering dared not remain long in waters he knew would soon be choked with ice, so he turned back.

His return to St. Petersburg, five years after he had left it, was not met with the praise and adulation he might have expected. Instead, he was criticized for not risking his ships and men to obtain final proof that a passage between Asia and North America existed. By then the Russians had recognized that ignorance of Arctic geography was not

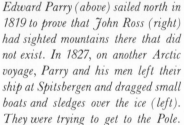

Edward Parry (above) sailed north in 1819 to prove that John Ross (right) had sighted mountains there that did not exist. In 1827, on another Arctic voyage, Parry and his men left their ship at Spitsbergen and dragged small boats and sledges over the ice (left). They were trying to get to the Pole.

only a scientific gap but a strategic danger. Bering's caution was interpreted as cowardice, and his expedition was considered a failure.

Fortunately, Bering had friends at court who supported his plea for a chance to redeem himself on another expedition. After more delays he again made the arduous trip across Siberia, arriving at Okhotsk in the fall of 1734. To his surprise, the frontier settlement he had seen on his first visit was now a teeming township overflowing with colonists and Russian government officials. Here, Bering got involved in all the red tape of an inefficient government that was trying to rule newly opened territories. He had to wait six years before he could get two ships built and manned. In 1740 he finally set sail, heading eastward this time, toward America.

His course took him parallel to the Aleutians and then to the Alaska mainland where he sighted volcanic Mount St. Elias and landed on Kayak Island. But, as Bering and most of his crew were beginning to suffer from scurvy, the expedition headed back after spending only one day on Alaska shores. Homeward bound, Bering's ship was wrecked

A splendid display of northern lights illumines the Arctic sky and three Eskimos (lower left) do a native jig in this fanciful representation of the discovery of the North Magnetic Pole. James Clark Ross, a young explorer and a student of magnetism, plants the British flag on a promontory that was the exact site of the Magnetic Pole. He had been sailing in Arctic waters with his uncle, John Ross, when their ship became iced in near the east coast of Somerset Island. During the long waiting period James had sledged to King William Island, where he made his historic discovery. To commemorate the event he later built a cairn on the coast of the island because, as he explained, "nature had erected no monument to denote the spot which she had chosen as the center of her great and dark powers."

in fog and rain on the beach at Bering Island, near Kamchatka. The crew was marooned there nine months before they were found, but Bering did not live to see the rescue.

Bering's achievements are among the most significant in the annals of Arctic exploration, for he cleared up many doubts and fears about the actual geography of Northeast Asia and Northwest America. Also, but more indirectly, he affected the future course of Arctic exploration. For, in the East, as it had been in the West, exploration was the prelude to colonization and trade. Now Russia's expanding imperialism followed the route of her explorers across the Bering Strait and down the North American coast. By the early nineteenth century, when she was firmly established in Alaska and had advanced as far south as San Francisco, Russia had become a threat to the other great colonial powers of the world.

This threat figured importantly in Britain's decision to resume the search for a northwest passage. By sending ships into northern waters once again, Britain wanted to discourage Russia from trying to take control of any portion of Arctic Canada. At the same time, Britain hoped to solve a serious unemployment problem for her navy. In 1815, at the close of the Napoleonic Wars, the British had an abundance of superbly trained officers and men, as well as a surplus of ships, yet had no way to use them. Resuming the quest for a northern route to the East appeared to be the best way to satisfy several objectives.

The first attempt began in 1818 with a two-pronged assault. One pair of ships was to sail between Greenland and Spitsbergen—proceeding toward the Bering Strait by way of the North Pole. Two other ships would try to reach the strait by sailing between Greenland and Northern Canada.

The course set by the first two ships indicates that many people still believed the North Pole to be surrounded by an ice-free ocean. The ships made little headway; they barely escaped disaster in a violent storm and were battered fiercely by the ice floes on their retreat to Spitsbergen. Second in command of this half of the expedition was Lieutenant John Franklin. His later exploits, like so many Arctic voyages, were destined to be marked by tragedy.

John Ross commanded the other half of the expedition, and his ships were more successful. Sailing up Davis Strait, he verified William Baffin's discoveries, which had been virtually forgotten. Pushing through Baffin Bay, Ross's

The Last Expedition of Captain Sir John Ross, R.N., HUISH, 1835

squadron "rediscovered" Smith, Jones, and Lancaster sounds. And Ross sailed as far as possible into Lancaster Sound, for he hoped to learn whether that opening would lead to a northwest passage.

After one day of exploration, a curious event took place. Ross halted the expedition because he said he saw mountains ahead, barring the way. The "mountains" were undoubtedly a weather phenomenon—perhaps a low-hanging curtain of fog—and most of Ross's junior officers wanted to sail on. But, certain of what he saw, Ross ordered the ships to turn around and return home.

The mysterious mountains plagued Ross in England and all but ruined his career. There were even malicious hints that he had found it convenient to see mountains just when he wanted to turn back. At last, to settle the controversy, the Admiralty dispatched another expedition in 1819. Leading it was Lieutenant Edward Parry, the young officer who had been Ross's second-in-command.

Parry quickly proved that the mountains did not exist, and his two-ship expedition continued to sail west, maneuvering through the narrow waters that lay between the pack ice and solid land. Then, zigzagging north and south to avoid the perilous floes, Parry moved on through bodies of water that he named Barrow Strait and Melville Sound. After passing the southernmost point of Melville Island, his ships were stopped by deep, solid pack ice covering the sea ahead. The expedition was forced to winter in a small harbor to wait for a passage to open through the ice.

All the next summer the long wait continued. Another Arctic autumn was approaching, with still no break in the ice to the west. Estimating that the floes were still as much as fifty feet thick, Parry ordered the expedition to pull back and return to England.

Parry's voyage was the first deep penetration of the confusion of channels and islands north of Canada. It was also the first wintering in the Arctic by British navy ships and was remarkably successful in terms of the good health and high spirits of the men.

Parry made two other attempts to find a northwest passage, but in these he was not so fortunate. His second try was made through Hudson Strait. After passing through the strait, his ships were caught in the ice of Foxe Basin and held for two winters before he could break them loose and return to England, his crew sick with scurvy. Parry's third attempt, through Lancaster Sound, ended quickly and disastrously when one of the two ships was wrecked on

In 1847 an Arctic council was established in England to try to determine the fate of the Franklin expedition. Included in the council membership were men like Edward Parry (second from left), James Clark Ross (fourth from left), and Leopold McClintock (third from right). Staring down from the wall behind the distinguished group are portraits of Sir John Franklin (left) and the man who backed the lost expedition, Sir John Barrow (right).

Somerset Island. (See detailed map on page 56.)

The Admiralty, which in 1818 had assaulted the Arctic as though it were an enemy line of battle, now called a halt to further exploration by ships of the Royal Navy. Parry did lead another Arctic venture, though. In 1827, starting from Spitsbergen, he and his men tried to reach the North Pole by pulling small boats fitted out with runners. The drift of the ice was not known then, so there were days when the party was carried farther south by ocean currents than it could move northward. In spite of this, and despite the exhausting labor of dragging the heavy boats over upended ice floes, the expedition reached 82°45' north, less than five hundred nautical miles from the Pole. This was a record that would stand for almost half a century.

One of the junior officers on the Parry expeditions was Commander James Clark Ross, who later discovered the Ross Sea and the Ross Ice Shelf in Antarctica. Commander Ross was also along when his uncle, Captain John Ross, set out in 1829 to have another go at the northwest passage in hope of repairing his reputation, which had been dimmed by his imaginary mountains.

The 1829 expedition was financed privately, for the British government had stopped investing in polar enterprises for the time being. John Ross's ship was the *Victory*. She was the first steamship ever to make a polar voyage; however, the voyage was not a very successful test of steam power.

First of all, the great, expensive steam engine proved almost useless in propelling the ship. Second, the engine and the stores of fuel filled so much space—and took up so much of the weight limit—that only a minimum of food and supplies could be taken along. Neither Ross nor any of his twenty-two-man crew was prepared for a long voyage, but this one turned out to be one of the most protracted polar expeditions in history.

Captain Ross reported later that, once out at sea, he had been forced "to consider [the *Victory*] as aught more than a sailing vessel," although she was rigged inadequately for this purpose. To reduce her load, the captain finally ordered that the engine be dismantled, and his men tossed parts of it overboard. Thus lightened, the *Victory* proceeded on through Baffin Bay until she became iced in near the east coast of Somerset Island.

Two years later Ross and his men abandoned their ship and went on by sledge. The next summer they built up their dwindling food supply by raiding the stores of a wrecked ship that had been left behind nine years earlier by Parry. They finally reached Lancaster Sound in August, 1833, and were picked up by a whaler bound for England. Thus, after four years in the Arctic, Captain Ross and nineteen of his original twenty-two men returned to a world that had given up all of them for dead.

The captain's nephew, James Clark Ross, did not idle away his four years with the expedition. He studied living habits of the Eskimos, the way they dressed, and the way they built their igloos. And frequently he sledged across the iced-over waters on exploratory journeys. In May, 1831, on one of these journeys, he made the expedition's most important discovery—the North Magnetic Pole. It is this iron-rich region, not the geographical North Pole, toward which the compass needle points.

In the 1840's the prestige-conscious British navy turned its attention once again to the Arctic and to the search for a northwest passage. At this time both the United States and Russia had active, imaginatively led navies. It seemed almost certain that ships of one of these two nations would complete the passage unless the Royal Navy acted swiftly.

Aside from this important political consideration, the Admiralty also had a technical interest in sending an expedition to the North once again. The screw propeller had been developed; now it was feasible for the navy to consider converting completely from canvas to steam. And, so far as the Admiralty was concerned, the Arctic was the most rigorous testing ground available.

James Clark Ross was asked to command the 1845 expedition because of his successful voyages of discovery in Antarctica. He had promised his wife that his days as a polar explorer were over, so he refused the assignment. It finally went to John Franklin, by then Sir John Franklin, who recently had been governor of the British territory of Tasmania. Franklin used Ross's ships, the *Terror* and the *Erebus*. They had already been strengthened for navigation in the icy polar seas. Now they were worked over again in the shipyards and reinforced further. Engines and screw propellers were installed, and the ships were provided with an emergency supply of coal to run them for twelve days.

The vessels were as comfortably and completely fitted out as was possible within the limits allowed by the tradition-bound Royal Navy. Officers' wardrooms were supplied with cut glass, china, and heavy Victorian silver. Libraries were stocked with more than twelve hundred books, and each ship had a barrel organ which, when cranked by hand, could play a variety of fifty tunes. Unfortunately, there was a complete lack of such Arctic essentials as sledges, snowshoes, tents, and extra-warm winter clothing. This expedition apparently was expected to travel through the Arctic while having little actual contact with it.

No one was worried, however. Britain, in the midst of a love affair with her navy, said good-bye to the expedition with an easy mind. The officers and men, 129 all told, were as fine a group as the navy had ever assembled. If there was a northwest passage to be found, Franklin and his men would find it. Everyone was certain of that.

The expedition was equipped for three years' sailing, but this represented precaution, not expectation. Many were confident that the *Terror* and the *Erebus* would reach Bering Strait in a single season and come back shortly thereafter. Yet the first winter passed, and the second one came—and still the ships did not return. A few voices suggested sending out a relief expedition. But the Admiralty,

Franklin won fame from his early Arctic voyages. Here are officers from his second expedition—top-hatted, the very models of British fashion—paddling a boat through a series of fantastic ice forms.

recalling the four-year hibernation of John Ross, scoffed at the idea that Franklin might be in trouble. So more time slipped by. Finally, when increasing worry throughout the nation made some action seem imperative, James Clark Ross was sent out with two ships to investigate. By then it was the summer of 1848, three years since Franklin's departure.

Ross spent a year off Somerset Island, sending out sledging parties to look for traces of the lost convoy. They found nothing. Their report of failure thoroughly alarmed the British, and the Admiralty was at last forced into large-scale action.

In the summer of 1850 a fleet of ships converged on the maze of islands and channels in which, somewhere, the men of Franklin's expedition were presumed to be lost. Three navy ships came from the west through Bering Strait and seven from the east through Lancaster Sound. Lady Franklin herself had appealed to the world for its prayers and its help. Her appeal brought five more ships to join the search. To supplement this armada, the Hudson's Bay Company sent Dr. John Rae, an experienced land explorer, to look along the northern rim of North America in areas difficult to reach by ship. Forty separate expeditions would be sent out before the search was ended—six of them by land, the rest by sea.

The first trace of the lost expedition was found in August, 1851, when an American search party reached tiny Beechey Island, which is just off the southwest coast of Devon Island in Barrow Strait. There the party stumbled onto the debris of a former campsite and found gravestones that bore the roughly carved names of three of Franklin's crew members. That was all. Nothing more was found of the lost expedition for another three years. By then it would have been a miracle if Franklin or any of his men were still alive; their store of provisions would have been exhausted long before.

The search continued, nevertheless—over hundreds of miles of pack ice and along thousands of miles of icy shores. Searchers often trapped Arctic foxes and put collars on them before releasing them. Attached to the collars were instructions that would tell the Franklin survivors the location of food caches that had been left for them.

In March, 1854, having grown weary of the search, the Admiralty announced that Sir John and his men were presumed to have perished in the service of the queen. Thus the case was closed—but it was reopened the following

In 1850, five years after Franklin began his fateful final voyage, rewards were offered to persons who could help solve the mystery of the lost expedition.

Sir John Franklin was considered too old to go to the Arctic again, but his friend Parry wrote the Admiralty: "He is a fitter man to go than any I know, and if you don't let him go, the old man will die of disappointment."

October when Dr. Rae returned from his long and tedious land search.

The explorer reported that he had met a group of Eskimos who had seen a large party of white men on King William Island three or four years earlier. The men had been observed moving south, dragging their boats as they traveled. Dr. Rae was led to the place where the white men had camped.

About thirty of them lay dead. Dr. Rae wrote in his report that "from the mutilated state of many of the corpses and the contents of the kettles, it is evident that our miserable countrymen had been driven to the last resources."

The report did not make Rae popular. England did not want to think that any extremity could reduce men of her idolized navy to cannibalism. The Admiralty was even more unhappy that the complete breakdown of the iron discipline on which it prided itself had been revealed to the world. It paid John Rae the ten thousand pounds that had been offered for discovering the fate of the Franklin expedition, possibly with the hope that the tragedy would now be forgotten. If so, it reckoned without Lady Franklin.

By this time she had become a romantic symbol to most of Britain. A popular ballad helped to dramatize her plea that the search be continued. It went, in part:

> In Baffin's Bay where the whale-fish blows,
> Is the fate of Franklin—no one knows.
> Ten thousand pounds would I freely give,
> To learn that my husband still did live.
>
> And to bring him back to a land of life,
> Where once again I would be his wife . . .
> I would give all the wealth I ere shall have,
> But I think, alas, he has found a grave.

When the Admiralty declined to make any further investigations, her successful appeal for private assistance enabled her to acquire and refit a small steam yacht, the *Fox*. In command of the *Fox* was Captain Leopold McClintock, whose services Lady Franklin had obtained from the navy with the help of Prince Albert, the husband of Queen Victoria.

McClintock had taken part in James Clark Ross's 1848–49 expedition, the first to look for Franklin, and had spent much time in the Arctic since then. His willingness to learn new ways distinguished him from most of his fellow officers. The standard Royal Navy method of maneuvering over Arctic ice was to use heavy sledges hauled by man power. Parry

Lady Franklin never lost hope that her husband would return.

OVERLEAF: *For years ships of exploration from many nations probed the narrow channels of Arctic seas, searching for some sign of Franklin.*

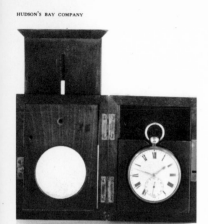

Franklin used the above chronometer on an early Arctic expedition. His attempt to complete the northwest passage is one of the routes that is traced on the Arctic map below.

had found this to be a slow and brutally exhausting way to travel—especially where pressure had pushed the floes into high, jumbled ridges. McClintock experimented, building lighter sledges, trying new types of clothing, observing how the Eskimos traveled. In the winter of 1859, when the *Fox* was held immovable in the pack ice, McClintock and his party headed for King William Island, where Dr. Rae reported the tragedy had occurred.

On the island McClintock found a number of relics of the Franklin expedition, including uniform buttons, tools and weapons made from a ship's wooden and metal fittings, and pieces of wardroom silverware bearing the monograms of Franklin and some of his officers. Moreover, from his talks with various bands of Eskimos, McClintock was able to piece together an account of how the lost expedition had probably met its end.

The Eskimos recalled seeing two ships caught in the ice just west of the northern tip of King William Island. Crushed by the tremendous pressure of pack ice, one ship

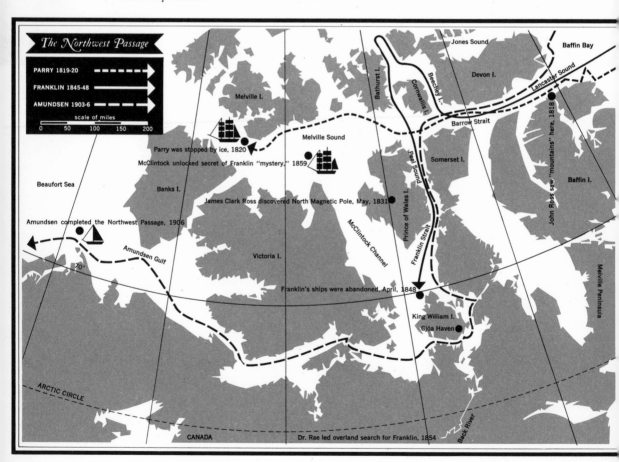

The Northwest Passage

PARRY 1819-20
FRANKLIN 1845-48
AMUNDSEN 1903-6

scale of miles
0   50   100   150   200

Jones Sound
Baffin Bay
Devon I.
Bathurst I.
Cornwallis I.
Beechey I.
Lancaster Sound
Melville I.
Barrow Strait
Melville Sound
John Ross saw "mountains" here, 1818
Parry was stopped by ice, 1820
McClintock unlocked secret of Franklin "mystery," 1859
Somerset I.
Baffin I.
Beaufort Sea
Banks I.
James Clark Ross discovered North Magnetic Pole, May, 1831
Prince of Wales I.
Franklin Strait
Amundsen completed the Northwest Passage, 1906
Amundsen Gulf
Victoria I.
McClintock Channel
Melville Peninsula
70°
Franklin's ships were abandoned, April, 1848
King William I.
Gjöa Haven
ARCTIC CIRCLE
CANADA
Dr. Rae led overland search for Franklin, 1854
Back River

One of Franklin's ships, the Erebus, *is shown in this painting by François Musin. The vessel is about to be trapped in the ice in Victoria Strait, near King William Island.*

had sunk before the natives could salvage anything from her, but the other had been cast up on the beach, badly broken. The ships' crews had abandoned the vessels and moved south. They had followed the shore line of King William Island, the natives said, taking their boats with them. Then they had moved toward the "large river" (the Back, or Great Fish River) that empties into the sea south of the island.

McClintock circled most of King William Island and sledged into the frozen estuary of the Back River. He left his second-in-command, Lieutenant Hobson, to explore the northwestern part of the island near the spot where the ships were said to have been locked in the ice. Following the shoreline that the retreating men must have traveled, McClintock and his party came on a bleached skeleton lying face down on a wind-swept gravel ridge.

"This victim was a young man," wrote McClintock ". . . [who] seems to have selected the bare ridgetop as affording the least tiresome walking, and to have fallen on his face in the position in which we found him."

On rejoining Lieutenant Hobson, McClintock learned

In 1853 Dr. Elisha Kent Kane led an American expedition to look for Franklin. West of Greenland his men chopped at thickening floes to let their ships advance through the ice. When the vessels were abandoned, Kane and his men rowed small boats to Greenland where a rescue party picked them up.

58

that his junior officer had found the first written record of the lost expedition. A tin box in a stone cairn had contained a brief message indicating that the expedition had spent its first winter on Beechey Island after circumnavigating Cornwallis Island. At the time the message was written—May 28, 1847—the two ships had just completed a winter in the ice off King William Island. All was well. (A photograph of the message is on page 60.)

However, an additional entry dated eleven months later had been written around the margins. All was well no longer. By then the expedition had lost nine officers and fifteen men. It had just abandoned its ice-bound ships and was starting toward the Back River, apparently with the forlorn hope of walking across the Canadian wilderness for hundreds of miles to a Hudson's Bay Company outpost. Sir John Franklin had died the previous summer.

McClintock's report to Lady Franklin explained the mystery of the lost ships to the satisfaction of most people. The main outlines were clear enough. In its second summer the Franklin expedition had sailed down Peel Sound and Franklin Strait. It had been beset by ice off King William Island and held immovable while the three-year food supply dwindled. There, Franklin had died, and Captain Francis Moira Crozier, his second-in-command, had taken over. Finally, on April 22, 1848, almost three years after leaving England, all hands had abandoned the ice-wracked ships and headed south on the melancholy march whose route was marked with their bones.

With this news the search for Franklin ended officially, but two years later private attempts were being made to fill in the missing details of the tragedy. Many of these attempts were made by Americans.

Dr. Elisha Kent Kane, an American surgeon who had explored the Philippines in his youth, requested backing for an expedition that would combine a further search for Franklin with an attempt to reach the North Pole. Reaching the Pole was his main objective, although it had less popular appeal than the Franklin search. By joining the two objectives he had little difficulty raising the money he needed to make the voyage.

Kane did not reach the Pole, but, sailing northward, he explored the west coast of Greenland and named Kane Basin. His book, *Arctic Explorations*, won him widespread acclaim and earned him status as "the outstanding American polar idol of the mid-century" despite his failure to contribute more to the Franklin story.

Dr. John Rae (above) and Leopold McClintock (below) helped most in solving the Franklin mystery.

H. M. S.hips Erebus and Terror

28 of May 1847 { Wintered in the Ice in Lat. 70°5' N Long. 98°23' W

Having wintered in 1846–7 at Beechey Island in Lat 74°43'28" N. Long 91°39'15" W after having ascended Wellington Channel to Lat 77° and returned by the West side of Cornwallis Island

~~Commander.~~

Sir John Franklin commanding the Expedition

All well

WHOEVER finds this paper is requested to forward it to the Secretary of the Admiralty, London, *with a note of the time and place at which it was found*: or, if more convenient, to deliver it for that purpose to the British Consul at the nearest Port.

QUINCONQUE trouvera ce papier est prié d'y marquer le tems et lieu ou il l'aura trouvé, et de le faire parvenir au plutot au Secretaire de l'Amirauté Britannique à Londres.

CUALQUIERA que hallare este Papel, se le suplica de enviarlo al Secretario del Almirantazgo, en Londrés, con una nota del tiempo y del lugar en donde se halló.

EEN ieder die dit Papier mogt vinden, wordt hiermede verzogt, om het zelve, ten spoedigste, te willen zenden aan den Heer Minister van de Marine der Nederlanden in 's Gravenhage, of wel aan den Secretaris der Britsche Admiraliteit, te London, en daar by te voegen eene Nota, inhoudende de tyd en de plaats alwaar dit Papier is gevonden geworden.

FINDEREN af dette Papiir ombedes, naar Leilighed gives, at sende samme til Admiralitets Secretairen i London, eller nœrmeste Embedsmand i Danmark, Norge, eller Sverrig. Tiden og Stœdit hvor dette er fundet önskes venskabeligt paategnet.

WER diesen Zettel findet, wird hier-durch ersucht denselben an den Secretair des Admiralitets in London einzusenden, mit gefälliger angabe an welchen ort und zu welcher zeit er gefundet worden ist.

Party consisting of 2 Officers and 6 Men left the Ships on Monday 24th May 1847

Gm. Gore Lieut.

Chas F. Des Voeux mate

…1848. HMS hips Terror and Erebus were deserted on the 22nd April 5 leagues NNW of this having been beset since 12th Sept 1846. The officers & crews consisting of 105 souls – under the command of Captain F.R.M. Crozier landed here – in Lat 69°37'42" Long 98°41' This paper was found by Lt Irving under the cairn supposed to have been built by Sir James Ross in 1831 – 4 miles to the Northward – where it had been deposited by the late Commander Gore in ~~May~~ June 1847. Sir James Ross' pillar has not however been found and the paper has been transferred to this position which is that in which Sir J. Ross' pillar was erected — Sir John Franklin died on the 11 June 1847 and the total loss by deaths in the Expedition has been to this date 9 Officers & 15 men.

James Fitzjames Captain HMS Erebus

F R M Crozier Captain & Senior Offr and start on tomorrow 26th for Backs Fish River

In 1860, an American with no experience as an explorer and no scientific knowledge set out hoping to solve another phase of the puzzling Franklin mystery. He was Charles Francis Hall, a poor but ambitious printer from Cincinnati, whose forays into the Arctic were often one-man operations.

Hall spent several years traveling and inquiring among the Eskimos, probing their memories instead of searching for relics. He learned that Captain Crozier and several of his men had finally gone to live with the Eskimos and had tried to adapt themselves to the Arctic. As a result, they had lived three or four years longer than their fellows. Then, becoming impatient of rescue, they had set out on a hopeless march toward civilization and disappeared forever.

If the native stories were true, Captain Crozier and the men who accompanied him were grim examples of what was needed to conquer the Arctic. It could not be overcome by men who tried to bring their own kind of life to it, complete with cut glass and monogrammed silver, but by those who could adjust their lives entirely to ice and snow and bitter cold.

Crozier and his companions realized this belatedly and stayed alive longer because of it. Dr. Rae, who spent years in the Arctic living like a native, knew it too. So did Captain McClintock, who learned to eat Eskimo food and to make long, rapid journeys on lightweight sledges. They were forerunners of men who would soon make polar history in both the North and the South.

On the west coast of King William Island, McClintock's men came upon a stone cairn (below). In it they found a paper (left) that told how the Franklin party had met its end.

CULVER PICTURES

IV THE TOP OF THE WORLD

Because of the lingering and far-reaching search for Franklin, the Canadian Arctic became a more widely explored area of the world. Yet, even in the late nineteenth century, vast reaches of northern Canada were still untraveled. Greenland too was largely a mystery. The interior of this huge island had never been penetrated, and a myth persisted that it contained not lifeless ice but grassy moors and rich soil in which crops might grow.

Exploration by the searchers for Franklin had shown that a northwest passage did exist—that there were, in fact, many ways to pass between the Canadian islands —but no ship had traversed it all the way. The northeast passage also awaited discovery, as it had since Barents was stopped by ice in the Kara Sea. And, like a great beacon, there was the North Pole itself, soon to become the most hard-sought goal of all.

The northeast passage was the first of the major prizes to be won, and it went with surprising ease to Baron Nils A. E. Nordenskiöld of Sweden. Nordenskiöld's expedition, which included the steam and sailing ship *Vega* and two cargo ships that were to accompany it part way, left Sweden in June, 1878. The voyage was smooth, untroubled by the hazards of floating ice. Skillful navigation was required, however, as the expedition was following an uncharted coastline most of the way and was plagued by thick fog.

The *Vega* came close to completing the entire passage in one season. When she was finally halted by the winter freeze-up, the Bering Strait lay only 120 miles away. The winter passed quietly, almost uneventfully. When the ice broke up at last, the *Vega* managed to reach the Bering Strait after just two days of sailing. The men were in perfect

The eerie monotony of Arctic sledging is shown at left in a work by Frank Wilbert Stokes, an artist who traveled with Robert Peary. At right is a picture of Fridtjof Nansen, taken after he tried to reach the Pole in 1896.

health, and the ship was undamaged. Thus, undramatically, after more than three hundred years, the northeast passage was completed.

Subsequent exploration at the top of the world did not proceed so smoothly, certainly not that of the Norwegian Fridtjof Nansen. His voyage became one of the classics of Arctic adventure. It was Nansen's theory that ice in the Arctic Ocean drifted in a constant direction from Siberia across the region of the Pole and down between Greenland and Spitsbergen, where it eventually melted. Nansen believed that a ship entering the ice at the right place would be frozen in and then carried over the Pole.

Nansen's primary interest, at least at first, was to prove this theory of ice drift. He was a brilliant scholar whose scientific background included specialization in zoology, oceanography, astronomy, and mathematics. Yet his knowledge, however vast, was not all theoretical. In 1888 he had made the first crossing of the Greenland ice cap, proving that in his own quiet way he was an adventurer as well as a scientist.

Nansen's sturdy ship, the Fram *(left), was locked in Arctic ice in January, 1895. At left below are some Greenland Eskimos who visited the ship during her first winter of polar drift. The crew of the* Fram *is shown at right, posed on the ship's deck. Nansen is seated, second from the right.*

Nansen had become interested in the drift of polar ice after reading a newspaper article that discussed the ill-fated ship *Jeanette*. The *Jeanette* had carried an American expedition on a voyage of discovery in 1879. After passing through the Bering Strait, the ship had been crushed by the floes and had sunk. She had plunged through the ice just north of the New Siberian Islands in June, 1881. Three years later, bits of debris and scraps of clothing were found on an ice floe near the southern tip of Greenland. It was determined that the material had come from the spot where the *Jeanette* had gone down. The writer of the article, a Norwegian scientist, advanced the notion that the only way the floe could have got from one place to the other was by drifting over the Pole.

Intrigued, Nansen searched for other evidence to support this theory of polar drift. He learned that driftwood used by Eskimos in Greenland was believed to have floated down from Siberian rivers and over the Pole by way of the Arctic Ocean. And he read that a Danish scientist, exploring the west coast of Greenland, had found a throwing-stick that doubtless had been used by Siberian, rather than Greenland, Eskimos.

This evidence led Nansen to declare: "If a floe could drift right across the unknown region, that drift might be enlisted in the services of exploration." His proposal was greeted skeptically, but he succeeded in finding men of imagination to provide financial backing. In 1893 an expedition was finally readied.

The success of this voyage depended on the ship. Nansen

envisioned a sturdily built vessel whose sides sloped inward to such a degree that she could slip "like an eel out of the embraces of the ice." Thus, when the ice floes moved in to squeeze the ship, she would be forced upward by the pressure and left resting on top of the floes. A ship of this design was built for Nansen by a Scottish ship architect. She was neat, compact, and strong, and she carried thirteen men. Nansen named her the *Fram*—which in Norwegian means "forward."

The *Fram* sailed from Christiania (now Oslo) in June, 1893. By September she had reached the New Siberian Islands and had nosed into the pack ice a short distance before being frozen in. The long drift began near the spot at which the *Jeanette* had gone down.

The *Fram* performed superbly, rising above ice floes that would have crushed any other ship. And Nansen's daily astronomical readings proved the soundness of his theory; the *Fram* and the entire frozen world in which she was locked were drifting northward across the top of the world. As time passed, however, it became apparent that the ship would pass near but not over the North Pole. Then the adventurer in Nansen got the upper hand of the scientist. He proposed that he and one companion leave the ship and travel by sledge to the Pole. It was a completely audacious undertaking; on March 14, 1895, eighteen months

Hoping to reach the Pole, Nansen left the Fram *and set off on land (above). He passed through a wilderness where polar bears roamed, his way brightened by northern lights as colorful as those in the Stokes painting at right.*

after the long drift had begun, he and Hjalmar Johansen said good-bye to the men of the *Fram* and headed north. With them went twenty-eight dogs, three sledges, two kayaks, and large stores of food.

Passage over the ice was treacherous almost from the start. The floes were upended into towering ridges so jagged that they overturned the sledges and slashed the skins of the kayaks. After twenty-three agonizing days, the men stopped. Exhausted, their food supply giving out, Nansen and Johansen decided to end the attempt. They were then at latitude 86°14′, farther north than any men had ever been. But they were still 226 nautical miles from the Pole.

When they left the *Fram*, the two men had talked confidently of being back in civilization within three months. But five months later they were nowhere near it. With August nearly passed, and with the sun sinking lower every day, it was plain that they would have to spend another winter in the Arctic. They stopped on a barren island in Franz Josef Land and built a stone hut on a hillside. There, with a larder of bear and walrus meat, and warmed by flickering walrus-blubber lamps, they passed the winter in a state of virtual hibernation. When the Arctic night ended, they were ragged, unkempt, and black with soot. But they remained in perfect health.

On May 19, 1896, they started south again, through the Franz Josef islands—traveling sometimes by sledge, sometimes by kayak. On one island they heard an incredible sound: off in the distance a dog was barking. They listened in wonder and disbelief as the sound cut through the Arctic stillness. When they heard a man's voice, they ran to investigate. By an improbable coincidence, in one of the world's loneliest regions, they had crossed paths with a British expedition led by the explorer Frederick Jackson.

Nansen and Johansen returned home aboard Jackson's ship. They arrived in Norway on August 13, 1896, and were acclaimed as national heroes. Nansen had proved his theory of polar drift, even though he had not reached the North Pole. On the day he returned to Norway, the *Fram* was just breaking out of the ice northwest of Spitsbergen. All thirteen members of the ship's crew enjoyed a tumultuous reunion in Norway some time later.

A year after the drift of the *Fram* had ended, a Swede named Salomon Andrée tried to reach the North Pole by air. With two companions he took off from Spitsbergen in a balloon named the *Eagle*. It was an elegant thing, made

Salomon Andrée was one of the first men to greet the Fram *at the end of her polar drift. He later tried to reach the North Pole in a balloon.*

After a winter-long drift, the Fram *emerged from the ice not far from Greenland, shown above in twilight colors. Nansen had left the ship by then. He and his companion often used a double kayak (right) on their way back from an attempt to reach the Pole.*

Andrée's idea of reaching the Pole by balloon was ridiculed in a Swedish magazine cartoon (above left). The balloon, the Eagle, is shown above, center, before Andrée took off. At right above is the balloon soaring over Spitsbergen.

of layers of silk, and its basket was woven of wicker and Chinese cane. Inside the basket were sledges, food, and survival gear so that an overland trip could be made from wherever the *Eagle* came down. After its takeoff the balloon soared northward and disappeared from sight. It was never seen again. For the next thirty-three years it belonged to the tragic realm of unsolved Arctic mysteries.

In 1930, by chance, the crew of a Norwegian scientific expedition stopped briefly at White Island, an outlying scrap of rock northwest of the Spitsbergen group. There they found the last camp of the Andrée expedition and the bodies of its men. In the camp were diaries and rolls of film that would yield an incredibly vivid flight record. Andrée's diary recounted how, after bucking shifting winds, the *Eagle* had stayed on course until ice on its gas-filled surface had brought it down three hundred miles northeast of the take-off point.

The men had started south in good spirits, according to their journals, sledging at first, but finally drifting on a large ice floe on which they built an igloo. Three polar bears and several seals provided plenty of fresh meat, so there was no real trouble until the floe began to break up as it neared White Island. The men went ashore and set up camp. Then, after a few more daily entries, the diaries ended. They gave no indication that the men were ill. And it was obvious that the men did not starve, for a large amount of food was found in the buried camp. Nor did they freeze, for they were dressed warmly and sleeping bags lay within their reach.

The mystery may never be solved beyond doubt, but the most widely accepted theory is that after prolonged exposure to sub-freezing temperatures while dragging their sledges over the ice, the men of the Andrée party simply died of exhaustion. There is another popular theory; it has been disputed, though not discounted, for many years. It suggests that the tragedy be blamed on the party's small Primus stove and on a tent made snugly airtight by snow sifting down around it. This theory indicates the men may have died of carbon monoxide poisoning.

Soon after the turn of the twentieth century, the northwest passage was finally completed—by a Norwegian, Roald Amundsen. He was twenty-nine, and his only previous polar experience had been as a member of a Belgian expedition that was the first to winter in Antarctica.

Amundsen hoped that conquering the northwest passage would enable him to reach the North Pole. But, since

The photograph below was taken after the Eagle *crashed on the ice.*

71

Roald Amundsen was a shrewd young Norwegian whose great seamanship helped him achieve his first polar goal, the conquest of the northwest passage.

the passage no longer seemed to promise great wealth, the expedition he proposed to backers was one that would make scientific observations at the North Magnetic Pole. Thus he was able to obtain some financial support because of the growing interest in science. He still found it necessary, however, to sail secretly from Christiania Harbor at midnight and in a driving rain to avoid having his ship seized by an impatient creditor.

Amundsen's vessel, the *Gjöa*, was so small that her total complement was only six men. She left Norway in June, 1903, and at first followed the route of the Franklin expedition. Then, proceeding down the eastern side of King William Island, Amundsen finally brought his ship into winter quarters in a snug harbor that is still labeled Gjöa Haven on many maps.

Here the expedition spent two winters, exploring and charting unmapped coastal regions as well as making scientific observations. On August 13, 1905, the *Gjöa* resumed her voyage. Of the many combinations of channels that formed possible passages to the North, Amundsen chose one that followed the upper edge of the North American mainland. Here, studded with islands and reefs, the waters were so shallow that the *Gjöa* scraped bottom more than once and barely escaped disaster on sharp, gray rocks along the coast. Then she passed into waters that had been explored and charted by other ships, and her major troubles were over. Amundsen was forced to spend one more winter

Amundsen's ship, the Gjöa, *was so small that she could carry only six men. But she made a safe journey from Norway to the Pacific Ocean.*

in the North—near the mouth of the Mackenzie River—but the next summer he sailed easily through the Bering Strait to the Pacific, thus completing the passage.

Amundsen's voyage had great personal significance beyond his success in exploring the waterway. By observing the natives, as McClintock and James Clark Ross had done, he learned much about sledging, cold-weather clothing, and the feeding and handling of Arctic dogs. He put this knowledge to good use on future expeditions, as did other explorers as well.

Amundsen went on to win the race to the South Pole, but that was merely a consolation prize. His primary polar goal, the one on which he had set his heart, had always been the North Pole. But this prize was won by Robert E. Peary. Thus to Amundsen the Arctic finally rendered not

glory but a very special kind of tragedy—the sense of personal failure.

If sheer doggedness of purpose can be a measure of a man's right of achievement, then Peary, more than any other man, deserved to reach latitude 90° north. He was a man utterly obsessed by a single desire: to stand briefly on the frozen desert at the top of the world. Reaching the Pole was for him the culmination of twenty-three years of striving.

Peary was an American naval officer whose interest in the Arctic was coupled with his desire to become world famous. As a young man he had made up his mind that Arctic exploration and the winning of the Pole offered the best means for achieving renown. He made his first expedition to Greenland in 1886, and thereafter he was firmly wedded to the Far North. For years he gave almost undivided attention to studying and perfecting Arctic travel methods and equipment. Sledges, dog harnesses, concentrated foods, stoves, shelters—nothing, not the smallest detail, escaped his attention.

With his 1898 expedition, Peary announced for the first time that the North Pole was his real objective. His quest did not have a very auspicious beginning, for his initial attempts to reach the Pole were failures. Through them, however, he was able to refine the techniques that would take him eventually to his goal.

He enlisted Eskimos in his expeditions, taking entire villages along with him. The women made clothing from seal and walrus skins, while the men served as sledge drivers, igloo builders, and trail makers. Peary's method of moving across the ice revolutionized Arctic sledging procedures. He would send a small advance party ahead of the main expedition to chop through the ice and blaze a trail. It was a grueling task, so the groups that made up the advance party were rotated constantly. In this way Peary was able to conserve the strength of both his dogs and his men.

In 1908, in the midst of a July heat wave, Peary left New York on his fourth attempt to reach the Pole. His ship, the *Roosevelt*, had been built for an earlier Peary expedition. On the northern coast of Greenland he picked up forty-nine Eskimos and 246 dogs and took aboard more than sixty tons of odorous whale and walrus blubber to feed the dogs. Then the *Roosevelt* headed up Smith Sound and Kennedy Channel between Greenland and Ellesmere Island. Captain Bob Bartlett, the vessel's Newfoundland-born skipper, brought her through the ice-choked waters

Among the many attempts to reach the North Pole was the one led by a United States Army major, Adolphus W. Greeley, in 1882. The expedition was a disaster, and Greeley and other survivors were not rescued until 1884. The drama of the rescue was captured in this painting by Albert Operti.

to 82°30′ north, a record for a ship steaming under her own power. From this point supplies were sledged another ninety miles to the take-off base at Cape Columbia, northernmost point of Ellesmere Island and 413 nautical miles from the Pole.

On February 28, 1909, the advance unit—Bob Bartlett and two Eskimos with their dogs and sledges—headed north across the frozen sea. The next morning the four main divisions set out with Peary's group in the rear. In all there were nineteen sledges with twenty-four men and 133 dogs. Seventeen members of the party were Eskimos, six were white, and one—Matthew Henson—was a Negro. For years Henson had been Peary's servant. But by now he had become a first-rate handler of dog teams, almost as skilled as an Eskimo.

On the second day out, the expedition was stopped by a black expanse of open water, a channel a quarter of a mile wide. Igloos were built; Peary resigned himself to wait, hoping that the channel would soon close. During the day one of the men slipped on the ice and fell into the freezing water. The presence of shelter and the availability of warm, dry clothing saved his life. And Peary held the man's icy feet to his own bare chest to warm them.

That night the channel closed with a loud crashing of floes. Quickly the men hitched the dog teams to the sledges and drove them—as fast as they could go—across the thin, rubbery ice. The following day an even wider channel stopped the party and held it. Peary fumed in despair, recalling how often his previous, frustrating attempts to reach the Pole had been blocked by open water. Three days

On his many journeys to the North, Robert Peary observed the Eskimos, learning how to build igloos for shelter and how to make the best use of sledge dogs. This charcoal sketch of an Arctic encampment was drawn on the spot by Stokes during one of the early Peary expeditions.

Peary (above) was photographed on the Roosevelt's *deck. His servant, Matthew Henson (below), went with him on the final polar assault.*

passed, then four, then a week. Finally the channel froze sufficiently to permit Peary to make a crossing, and he hurried his men across.

By March 14, two weeks out, the bitter cold and the rough going had begun to take their toll. The first of Peary's exhausted men and the weakest dogs and Eskimos were sent back to the base at Cape Columbia. Soon, others followed. At last, only Peary, Henson, Bartlett, and the Eskimo drivers were left.

Bartlett, who had been cutting a trail through the ice, was ahead of the others. But they caught up when more open water stopped him. Together now, the group made camp and waited. During the night all were awakened by the crashing of ice. The area on which they were camped was breaking up. Bartlett found his igloo resting precariously on a floe that had broken loose and was floating away from the rest of the camp. He hitched up his dogs immediately, and as the floe bumped briefly against solid, anchored ice he drove the team forward across the moving line of contact. It was close. A moment later the floe drifted off into the blackness of the channels.

On April 1 Bob Bartlett made his last trail-blazing march. The next morning, exhausted, he left the expedition and started back. Now it was up to Peary—accompanied by Henson and four Eskimos—to complete the final 133-mile step to the Pole. Up to this point Peary had conserved his strength, saving himself every possible effort. Now he moved out to make his own trail.

Good fortune was with him on this last big push. Even the ice was good. Although pressure ridges frequently rose to a height of fifty feet, there was always a passage through them or a big packed snowdrift that provided a way over at just the right spot.

The temperature was about 30 degrees below zero, which is favorable weather for sledging, and the party pushed ahead, averaging twenty-five miles each day. Peary's great fear now was that another body of water would stop him just short of his goal. Although the ice looked solid, it rumbled and cracked in response to the irresistible urgings of currents and tides. At one point the men were forced to drive their sledge from floe to floe across a sea of drifting ice. Henson fell in when a floe tipped up under his feet. An Eskimo grabbed him just in time and pulled him out by the collar.

On April 6, Peary gave the signal to stop. He had a shield of snow blocks built for protection from the wind, and from behind this he took a careful sighting of the sun to determine his exact position. He calculated that he had reached latitude 89°57′ north, still three miles short of his goal. For the next thirty hours he marched around the area to make absolutely certain that he would pass over the point that marked the very top of the world. When this point was finally reached, he planted five flags in the ice, placed a strip of the American flag and a brief account of his journey into a jar, and took possession of the entire surrounding desolation for the United States.

"The Pole at last," he wrote. "The prize of three centuries. My dream and goal for twenty years." Then, in another document, he was careful to note that standing with him at 90° north were four Eskimos and "Matthew Henson, colored."

The return trip was swift and without incident, and the *Roosevelt*'s southward voyage went smoothly. But Peary did not return home to the acclaim he had expected. A few days before he announced his success from a wireless station

Peary's ship, the Roosevelt, *was stopped by ice in Kennedy Channel after going farther north than any ship steaming under her own power.*

in Labrador, another Arctic adventurer, Dr. Frederick A. Cook, had told the world a different story. Cook claimed that a full year earlier he and two Eskimos had reached the Pole and were only just returning from northern isolation to make the achievement known.

Peary knew Cook well enough; the anthropologist had been along on one of Peary's early expeditions across the Greenland ice. But Peary was astonished to find that at first Cook's story was believed and his was doubted. Cook could not prove he had reached the Pole—nor could Peary, as people were quick to point out. Bob Bartlett had turned back short of the Pole, and there was no one but

Matthew Henson to vouch for what had happened after that. In 1909 the testimony of a Negro did not count for very much.

As time passed, public opinion began to favor Peary. There were far too many holes in Cook's story, too many contradictions. But the issue was never completely laid to rest. For years afterward there were Arctic experts who held strong reservations as to whether Peary really did reach 90° north. Even today, when it constitutes far less than a burning issue, the question is occasionally raised.

Admiral Robert E. Peary was nearly fifty-three years old when he and his well-equipped American task force came back from the North Pole. He was certainly too old to start thinking about any more expeditions that would make new demands on his personal powers of endurance. But he did look toward the South Pole, and he made tentative plans to organize an Antarctic expedition. He would direct it, he said, but his good friend Bob Bartlett would be the man to drive on to the Pole itself.

The expedition never came into being. The South Pole was conquered by another man before Peary's claim on the North Pole had been firmly established. He received the recognition he had earned, finally. But it was his fate that by the time he was recognized for his unique accomplishment the prize seemed outdated and insignificant. The great era of north polar exploration had passed.

The desperate "home stretch" of Peary's race to the North Pole—over pressure ridges of ice that were sometimes piled as high as fifty feet—may be seen in the picture at left, painted by Harold von Schmidt. Peary's claim that he was the first to reach 90° north was challenged by Dr. Frederick Cook, whose adherents built an arch (at right) in Brooklyn, New York, to show that they believed him.

WE BELIEVE IN YOU

UNDERWOOD & UNDERWOOD

V MYSTERY OF THE SOUTHERN CONTINENT

It was not until the eighteenth century that men's curiosity about the uncharted regions around the South Pole began to match their interest in the North. Ever since the time of the Greeks, geographers had been certain that a southern continent existed, but the reasons advanced for it were unconvincing. Early geographers believed it was needed to balance the continents of the Northern Hemisphere. Added to this belief was the myth that the southern continent was a land of lush beauty and fabulous wealth. Thus Antarctica was assumed to extend far up into the warm latitudes, a conception that gradually shrank as explorers sailed deeper and deeper into the Southern Hemisphere and could find no great land mass.

Belief in the southern continent persisted so strongly, however, and among men of such stature and influence that in 1768 the British Admiralty decided to prove or disprove its existence. An expedition of two ships was later organized, with Captain James Cook as its leader. Cook was a man of rare abilities, exceptionally skilled in mathematics and astronomy, and probably the greatest navigator of his time. In naming him, the Admiralty had chosen well.

On July 13, 1772, the Cook expedition set sail from Plymouth, England. In December the men sighted the first of the tabular, or flat-topped, icebergs which later generations would recognize as Antarctic "landmarks." From that time on, fog, rain, snow, and gales complicated navigation through the ice.

On January 17, 1773, the ships passed over the Antarctic Circle, the first time that line had ever been crossed.

Captain James Cook

Adélie penguins are clustered in the foreground of this Antarctic land-and-seascape, preening and sunning. Behind them are the frozen mountains of Cape Hallett, which rise majestically above the ice-choked Ross Sea.

Actually, Cook crossed the Antarctic Circle three times during his circumnavigation of the globe, but each time the crowding ice floes prevented him from penetrating farther. It was only in the summer months that he could negotiate the ice-jammed waters of the south polar seas. Hence, Cook had to spend three years completing his voyage around the southern part of the world.

The discovery of any solid land in the Antarctic region almost eluded Captain Cook. Only at the close of his voyage did he come on South Georgia, a glacier-topped island whose only vegetation was moss, lichens, and some coarse grass. He also discovered a group of islands he named Sandwich Land (the South Sandwich Islands) after Britain's First Lord of the Admiralty.

Cook did not prove the existence of an Antarctic continent; he merely insisted that if there was such a land it would be inaccessible because of the barrier of ice around it. Moreover, he wrote: "I can be bold enough to say that no man will ever venture farther than I have done; and that the lands which may be to the south will never be explored." Thus James Cook closed the door on Antarctic exploration;

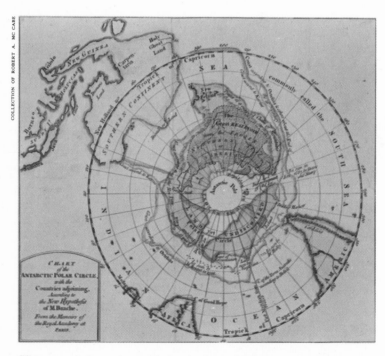

This map of Antarctica, with the Arctic superimposed, was published in 1763 to illustrate a theory that the South Pole lay under water. Another fantasy of that time, one that added to the glamour of polar exploration, was that every voyage was planned in an elegant drawing room (at right).

it would not be reopened until the nineteenth century.

A year after Captain Cook returned to England, the Admiralty invited him to lead a new polar expedition, this time to the North. His objective would be that familiar will-o'-the-wisp, the northwest passage. He was to attempt it from Bering Strait, sailing across the top of Alaska.

He set out in 1778, discovered what were known later as the Hawaiian Islands, and then pushed far up into the Bering Strait. At latitude 70°41′ north he was finally barred by ice that was piled twelve feet high and extended as far as he could see. The northeastern tip of Asia was near his ship, easily visible, and as the weather was clear, he could look eastward and see Alaska on the horizon. Half a century earlier a dense fog had prevented Vitus Bering from seeing both continents at once.

Cook lost his life on this expedition—but not on an ice-bound ship or in a frozen wilderness. Ice moving in on him

Captain Fabian von Bellingshausen sailed to the Antarctic for Russia.

Below is the celebrated meeting of Bellingshausen and Palmer in Antarctic waters; when fog lifted, Palmer found his sloop between two Russian ships.

Nathaniel Palmer was captain of an American seal-hunting expedition.

Voyages Round the World, FANNING, 1833

had discouraged him from continuing the search for a northwest passage, and he returned to the Hawaiian Islands; there he was killed in a fight with natives.

Despite the negative nature of Cook's findings, hope persisted that where there was land there was wealth. After Cook's explorations, the southern seas became the scene of almost feverish activity by hunters, true to the pattern that had been set in the North. Both of Cook's Antarctic land discoveries, South Georgia and the South Sandwich Islands, abounded in fur seals, however barren they were of vegetation. Around the time of the American Revolution, sealing crews became involved in a wholesale slaughter that reduced the enormous seal packs almost to extinction. Hunters added to their growing wealth and at the same time added island after island to the map as they widened their search for new herds to annihilate.

It was during the course of this search that a young American, Nathaniel Palmer, had a surprise encounter with Captain Fabian von Bellingshausen of the Imperial Russian Navy. Palmer's ship was the sloop *Hero*, a sealer out of Stonington, Connecticut. She was becalmed in heavy fog north of what was to be called Palmer Peninsula.

Palmer had sighted the tip of the peninsula, but America's belief that he was the first actually to see the Antarctic continent has been widely disputed. The Russians claim this honor for Captain Bellingshausen, and the British believe that William Smith and Edward Bransfield sighted the Antarctic continent several months before Palmer's landfall was made. Palmer himself never claimed to be first, but his voyage on the *Hero* brought him considerable fame—notably because of his chance meeting with Bellingshausen.

The *Hero* was one of a fleet of five ships that had been scouting among the ice-covered islands for fur seals when the wind subsided and fog rolled in. The time was early February, 1821, well past the middle of the brief Antarctic summer. The *Hero* was small, but if Captain Palmer experienced feelings of pride as his ship rode on the gray, sluggish swell, he could be excused. For he was only twenty-one, and New Englanders in that day did not give command of ships to men of any age who had not proved themselves. Whatever his thoughts, the young skipper was astonished, when the fog lifted, to find his ship lying between a frigate and a sloop of war. He ran up the American flag; the two other ships responded by hoisting the Russian colors. The frigate lowered a boat and sent the

The lordly bearing of James Clark Ross, as seen in his portrait at right, suggests that he may have spent a lifetime cloistered in offices of the Admiralty in London. Actually, he spent a great part of his life outdoors in sub-freezing temperatures, making important discoveries at both ends of the earth. Two of his Antarctic exploits are shown at left in watercolors painted on the spot by J. E. Davis. Above is a New Year's Day (1842) celebration held on an ice floe in the Ross Sea. Below are some of Ross's men landing on Possession Island, a rocky islet that swarmed with curious penguins. In 1822, long before Ross and his navy ships first journeyed to Antarctica, James Weddell, a British seal hunter, sailed farther into southern waters than anyone before him—an event that was preserved for all times in the luminous picture below.

compliments of Captain Bellingshausen and an invitation for young Palmer to come aboard. Palmer accepted.

Early American accounts of this meeting are largely fictional. They state that the Russian expressed amazement and chagrin at finding a young American in waters where he, Bellingshausen, had assumed he was making original discoveries. However, the Russian's own account of the meeting indicates that the two men talked about the sealing industry and little else.

Bellingshausen was just completing his explorations when he met the young American. The captain had left Russia a year and a half earlier on an expedition that was part of a growing revival of national interest in the polar regions. The British had withdrawn to the Arctic to take up the long-forgotten search for a northwest passage. Czar Alexander I of Russia had reacted to this by sending out two expeditions, one to look for the northwest passage—the other, under Bellingshausen, to explore the Antarctic.

Little is known of the Russians' northern expedition except that it failed in its purpose. As for Bellingshausen, he took his ships down the Atlantic to South Georgia where, before moving on, he made surveys of the south coast of the island—so accurate that they were being used until very recent years.

Britain's James Weddell

After wintering in warmer waters, the Russians headed southward again and on January 22, 1821, made history's first landfall inside the Antarctic Circle. It was a frigid chunk of steep-sided rock, which Bellingshausen named Peter I Island after a former czar. A month later the expedition sighted a section of Antarctic seacoast which the captain named Alexander I Island to honor the reigning czar. Shortly thereafter, Bellingshausen had his encounter with Palmer, and within a few days was homeward bound.

With the Russians' departure, the seal hunters were left in sole possession of the Antarctic. Like the whalers of the North, the sealers, with few exceptions, were inclined to keep their discoveries secret. One of these exceptions was the Enderby brothers. These British ship owners were responsible for much of the Antarctic exploration that took place between 1822 and 1839. The men hired to command their ships were often scientists as well as hunters, men willing to spend part of their time in the unprofitable business of gaining knowledge rather than searching for game. Such a man was the skipper James Weddell.

In 1822 Weddell headed south from the South Shetland

Islands to look for new sealing grounds. He found none, but he went 214 nautical miles farther south than Cook had gone. And he sailed into that great indentation in the Antarctic continent that was later named the Weddell Sea. Usually this body of water is so choked with pack ice as to be impenetrable to ships. But the sea was strangely free of ice that year. At one point, Weddell wrote in his log, in capital letters, "NOT A PARTICLE OF ICE TO BE SEEN."

Weddell's small ships were hardly suited to the dangers of Antarctic navigation, nor were they fitted out for anything other than sealing. But Weddell did what he could to make careful scientific observations. He took readings of sea-water temperature, observed water currents, and kept a record of ice form and movement.

With the stepped-up interest in science, Antarctica soon became the site of intense exploration. Between 1837 and 1843, France, Britain, and the United States each sent expeditions into southern waters.

The French left home in January, 1838, with two ships under the command of Jules S. C. D. d'Urville. His instructions were simple: to sail farther south than any other man, including Weddell, for the glory of France. D'Urville was unable to carry out these instructions to the letter because the Weddell Sea was impossible to enter. So he turned north to explore the warmer and less forbidding islands and waters of the South Pacific.

He returned to the Antarctic early in 1840, hoping to find the South Magnetic Pole, but he found only the sheer ice cliffs of the continent itself. He claimed a stretch of coast for France and named it Adélie Land in honor of his wife. (The Adélie penguins, the smaller of the two penguin species, were also named to honor Madame d'Urville.) He sailed home shortly afterward, and the French flag did not return to Antarctica for more than a century. But, because of d'Urville, France today claims a thin wedge of territory that extends from the coast of Adélie Land to the South Pole.

France's Jules S. C. D. d'Urville

The British expedition reached Hobart, Tasmania, in August, 1840, and headed for Antarctica three months later. Its commander was James Clark Ross, a veteran of six Arctic expeditions. He had reached the North Magnetic Pole several years earlier; now he hoped to perform a similar feat in the South. Ross's ships, the 370-ton *Erebus* and the 340-ton *Terror*, were the stoutest ever to sail the south polar seas. They had been strengthened to resist the ice, and they had water-tight compartments to keep them from sinking, even if pierced by the swiftly drifting floes.

Sailing southward along the line of longitude 170° east, Ross came up against a mountainous, ice-girt coast. He was profoundly disappointed, for he had hoped to find a water-way—perhaps a channel—that would lead him directly to the South Magnetic Pole. Ross followed the coastline until it swung sharply to the south, and at one point he paused on a rocky island to take possession of the territory for the British Crown. He named his discovery Queen Victoria Land. (See Antarctic map at back of book.)

Without realizing it, the explorer had sailed into a second sea-filled dent in the continent, the Ross Sea. Following the seacoast, his ships passed an island on which two tall mountain peaks were sighted. The peaks were named Mount Terror and Mount Erebus after Ross's ships. Mount Erebus proved to be a strange paradox—an active volcano in a frozen land, trailing a plume of smoke. Its pit was filled with fire; its flanks were icy, eternally cold.

Louis Le Breton, d'Urville's artist and surgeon, was so impressed by the planting of the French flag on Adélie Land that he sketched the scene—and included himself in it, standing on a rock (center).

Shortly after skirting the volcano, Ross found himself heading toward impenetrable land, and his hope of sailing to the Magnetic Pole was at last dashed completely. "As we approached the land under all studding sails," he wrote, "we perceived a low, white line extending from its eastern extreme point as far as the eye could discern to the eastward. It presented an extraordinary appearance, gradually increasing in height as we got nearer to it and proving at length to be a perpendicular cliff of ice, between 150 and 200 feet above the level of the sea, perfectly flat and level at the top and without any fissures or promontories on its own seaward face."

Ross had discovered what is known today as the Ross Ice Shelf. His ships sailed along it for days as he looked for a break in the ice, but there was none. The approach of winter sent the expedition back to Tasmania. The next summer Ross explored almost the entire length of the ice shelf, but the onset of another winter forced him to withdraw before he had definitely established its eastern limits.

The expedition spent a third year in the Antarctic, beginning a determined push southward into the Weddell Sea late in 1843. When the ships were stopped by pressure-heaped ice, Ross gave up and returned to England.

The British enterprise under Ross was the best prepared of the expeditions sent out at this time. The American expedition was undoubtedly the worst. In fact, it was perhaps the most poorly prepared expedition that ever sailed to Antarctica. Bad temper had marred every step of its planning for several years, and Navy officers assigned to the voyage had resigned in large numbers because of the feuds that developed.

Six vessels were allotted to the expedition. Three of them were warships, with open gunports that let in cold air and heavy seas. One of the three other ships was so slow that she was sent home long before nearing Antarctica. None of the ships had been strengthened to resist the pressure of pack ice, and much of the wood used to construct the ships soon became rotten.

To command this sad flotilla, the United States Navy selected Lieutenant Charles Wilkes, a competent enough seaman but the strictest kind of disciplinarian. He sailed south on August 18, 1838, accomplishing little during the first season because of extremely bad weather. A storm struck his fleet just off Cape Horn, and one of his smaller ships was sunk with all hands aboard.

The expedition wintered in Sydney, Australia, where

the populace came down to look with disbelief at ships so unprepared for the rigors of Antarctic travel. Wilkes did what he could to remedy the worst defects. He had cracks closed with tarred canvas and sheet lead, and wherever possible, the structural weaknesses of the ships were strengthened. Despite these attempts, Wilkes later wrote that "most of our visitors considered us doomed to be frozen to death."

Commanding four ships now, instead of the original six, Wilkes headed south again when the weather improved. He sighted the coast of Antarctica at or near Adélie Land, which d'Urville was claiming for France at about the same time. Then, sailing west, he took his ships along the mainland, past fifteen hundred miles of coastline, the portion now called Wilkes Land.

Treacherous ice battered Wilkes' frail ships as they navigated the coastal waters. Ice floes pressing against the sides of one ship smashed her rudder and threatened to destroy the ship completely. But she escaped destruction when favorable winds pushed her through the thickest ice into clear water again. There the carpenter's crew worked continuously for twenty-four hours to restore the broken rudder so that the ship could get back to Sydney for major repairs.

In January, 1840, medical officers of the *Vincennes*, the flagship of the expedition, reported to Wilkes that the crew was in such poor health that the ship should turn back at once. In an account of his voyage, Wilkes wrote that after weighing the doctors' recommendations, he "came to the conclusion, at whatever hazard to ship and crew, that it was my duty to proceed . . ."

As the voyage continued, Wilkes sighted land periodically, or at least that was what he thought. Actually, the ice fields kept his ships so far off the coast that there were long periods during which Wilkes could not have known for certain what was land and what was just another iceberg. In many instances Wilkes reported seeing land where later explorers saw only ocean. These particular lapses were taken more kindly in subsequent years, however, when it became known how the phenomenon called refraction is exaggerated in the polar latitudes. Because of refraction, land often appears to be many miles nearer than it actually is.

Charles Wilkes returned home expecting to be hailed as a successful explorer. But his claims of having sighted land were immediately disputed, and he was court-martialed on charges brought by his officers—centering mainly on the harsh treatment of his men. Wilkes was acquitted of most of these charges, but there is no doubt that he was a stern martinet. Of the 545 men who started the voyage or signed up en route, 127 deserted before it was over.

Despite the lack of preparation and the misfortunes of the voyage, this expedition accomplished a great deal with the means at hand. It was certainly no credit to the United States government that Wilkes was sent out with such a poorly planned, poorly equipped expedition. It seems likely that only a man of Wilkes' determination and hard-driving force could have accomplished so much under the circumstances. In any event, the ill will engendered by this expedition was such that the nation—and the government as well—lost interest in the south polar regions and had nothing more to do with them for an entire century. During this time, history in Antarctica was being made by British and European explorers, and the search for the South Pole became a fiercely waged contest, a test of determination, endurance—and heroism.

Narrative, WILKES, 1844

America's Charles Wilkes

G Hudyard...

VI THE RACE TO THE SOUTH POLE

In 1897 the steamship *Belgica* sailed south from Antwerp to carry out scientific observations along the western coast of Palmer Land. This was planned as a short expedition, but it lasted nearly a year. Commanding it was Lieutenant Adrien de Gerlache of the Belgian navy, a man whose measure of fame was to be achieved strictly through an error of judgment: he sailed too far south too late in the season. Thus his expedition became the first ever to spend a winter below the Antarctic Circle.

Among those on board the *Belgica* during this voyage was Roald Amundsen, who was then taking his first steps into the life of exploration he had chosen. Another member of the party was Dr. Frederick A. Cook, who would later cause Robert E. Peary a great deal of trouble.

Amundsen, the first mate, assumed virtual command of the ship when scurvy broke out among the men, and both de Gerlache and the ship's captain took to their beds—so ill that they made out their wills. A surgeon as well as an anthropologist, Dr. Cook bullied the men back to health by forcing them to eat seal and penguin meat, which most of them, himself included, detested.

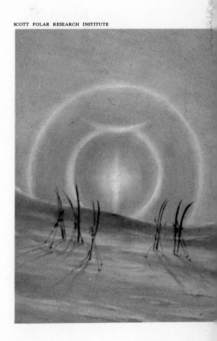

The *Belgica* was beset by ice in March, 1898, and remained locked in the floes for eleven months until she was freed with the help of explosives and ice saws. Even while she was breaking loose from the ice, a British expedition led by Carsten Borchgrevink, a Norwegian explorer, was unloading supplies on a rocky beach at Cape Adare, near the edge of the Ross Sea. This expedition won special fame by proving that it was possible to winter on the continent of Antarctica in reasonable comfort and safety. Borchgrevink's success set off a small but concentrated rush to the

Carsten Borchgrevink (left) and a generation of explorers who followed him found that Antarctica was habitable and had a rare beauty of its own (right).

Sailors in jaunty uniforms, members of Robert Falcon Scott's first south polar campaign, are shown below hauling their flag-bedecked sledge over the icy land-scape of Antarctica. Scott, Shackleton, and the expedition's artist and surgeon, Dr. Edward Wilson, are pictured at right.

south polar regions beginning in 1901 with the formation of three expeditions—Swedish, German, and British. The British venture was especially significant, for it began blazing a way that led eventually to the South Pole.

Most of the manpower for this expedition was supplied by the Royal Navy, which had assigned Robert Falcon Scott to lead it. Scott was an Englishman's ideal of what a naval officer should be—handsome, forthright, completely faithful to navy traditions. He was not an experienced polar explorer, however. As a matter of fact, he had not considered becoming involved in polar exploration until two days before he applied to command the expedition. Yet his knowledge of science was to prove advantageous to him, and he tried to compensate for his lack of polar knowledge by reading a great deal and by talking to men of practical experience.

The Scott party set up its Antarctic base at the western end of the Ross Ice Shelf. There the towering cliffs terminate in Ross Island, which contains the smoldering crater of Mount Erebus and the icy cone of Mount Terror. Between Ross Island and the mainland shore of Victoria Land is a sheltered opening called McMurdo Sound. There, in January, 1902, Scott anchored his ship, the *Discovery*, and the work of transferring supplies and dogs to the gravelly beach of Ross Island began.

Winter arrived some months later, and during this long, bleak period only routine weather observations could be carried out. When summer returned, Scott, along with Ernest Shackleton and the expedition's artist and surgeon, Dr. Edward Wilson, started south to explore the ice shelf. It was still unknown territory; only time would reveal its vast extent—a level expanse of ice, hundreds of feet thick. Parts of it floated, but much of its enormous bulk rested on the bottom of the sea. The three men would have occasion to learn more of the ice shelf's geography, frequently with considerable anguish.

Scott's support parties had already pushed on to lay the supply depots when he and his two companions set out with their dogs and sledges. A mysterious illness soon weakened the dogs and they had to be killed, one by one. This was but another of Scott's many experiences with dogs that reinforced his aversion to using them as work animals, an aversion that would have profound results in the future.

As the number of dogs dwindled, the men were reduced to hand-sledging. At 82°17' south, after fifty-nine days on the ice, they turned back; they were still more than four

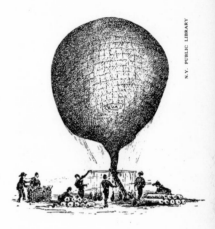

Eva, *a small army balloon, took Scott aloft during his first Antarctic expedition so he could survey the ice shelf.*

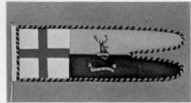

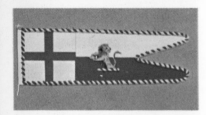

hundred nautical miles from the Pole, but none of them were feeling well. Dr. Wilson had detected the symptoms of scurvy on their gums and feet, and their joints had begun to stiffen. Shackleton, the biggest and most robust of the trio, was hardest hit, barely able to move and spitting up blood in continual coughing spells. When the men reached the *Discovery*, on the last shreds of endurance, Shackleton was in such poor shape that Scott had no choice but to send him home on a relief ship that had come during their absence. The rest of the party remained in the Antarctic for another year until the *Discovery* was finally freed from the ice. Then the expedition returned to England.

Little more than two years later, Shackleton surprised Scott and a great many others by announcing his decision to lead an expedition that would try to reach the South Pole. It was said that Shackleton's decision had been prompted by his deep chagrin at having been invalided during his sledging journey with Scott. Whatever the motivation, he obtained financial support for his expedition and was back in Antarctica by early 1908.

Shackleton brought two innovations to polar exploration. One was his invention of lightweight boxes to carry rations. The other was a motor vehicle modified for travel over ice and snow. Frankly experimental, this vehicle accomplished little beyond pulling sledges over the smooth, packed snow around the camp. But it proved that combustion engines could function in Antarctic cold, and it foreshadowed a later, mechanical age of polar exploration.

As his principal beasts of burden, Shackleton had chosen Siberian ponies. Like Scott, he disliked dogs, and though he brought some along, he planned to use them only for short hauls. And, also like Scott, he set up headquarters on the shores of McMurdo Sound.

Shackleton began his advance toward the Pole early in the spring, after a winter of preparations. Advance parties had laid supply depots for the first part of the 1,730-mile round trip, but for most of the trek Shackleton would have to subsist on the supplies he and his companions carried. Four men and four ponies started out on the march, but three of the animals gave out and had to be shot while the men were still on the ice shelf. As each pony was killed, the men ate what they could of its meat and put

Daring, courageous, intelligent—Robert Falcon Scott (right) seemed well qualified to fulfill England's polar ambitions. Three of the sledge flags used on Scott's south polar expeditions are shown above, painted by Wilson.

the rest in a frozen depot for possible use on their return.

As the men proceeded, the mountain range that had more or less paralleled their course swung across their path. Ordinarily, mountains as sheer as these would have been impassable, but Shackleton discovered a glacier that formed a kind of highway between two of the peaks. This glacier was the largest expanse of ice that men had ever seen, more than a dozen miles wide and a hundred miles long. Shackleton named it Beardmore Glacier—after the industrialist William Beardmore, who had provided much of the financial backing for this expedition.

Beardmore Glacier turned out to be a dangerous highway on which to travel. Deep crevasses had been made in the glacial ice by the stress of its gradual downhill movement. These crevasses were often concealed from view by a coating of fresh snow. The men climbed slowly and carefully, but they could not avoid toppling into some of the crevasses. However, by harnessing themselves to their sledges they made certain that when they did fall in, they could pull themselves out—safe from what otherwise would have meant inevitable death.

Once atop the polar plateau they found that the sledging surface was almost always bad, whether the snow was soft or frozen into the hard, wind-swept ridges called *sastrugi*. By this time clothing and shoes were wearing out, and frostbite was becoming more and more widespread. The mercury in thermometers stayed between 25 and 30 degrees below zero, which ordinarily were ideal temperatures for sledging. But now the cold was accompanied by blizzards that made travel arduous and often impossible.

On January 1, 1909, Shackleton decided that he and his men could not reach the South Pole. However, he was determined to push on for three more days. Then a blizzard came up, and howling winds of eighty to ninety miles an hour kept the men huddled in their tent, striving to keep warm in frozen sleeping bags. On January 9 the winds subsided, and the men marched south for a few more hours. When they finally stopped, they hoisted the British flag and took possession of the desolate land on which they stood. They were at latitude 88°23' south when they turned back, only ninety-seven nautical miles from the Pole.

The return trip was mostly downhill, but it was far from easy going. "It is neck or nothing with us now," Shackleton wrote. "Our food lies ahead and death stalks us behind." Starvation remained a threat even after the men had reached the line of depots, because there was

THE EASTERN PARTY

barely enough food in one depot to enable them to reach another. One day their breakfast consisted of a single biscuit apiece. Another day, when the food was scant, they dug into the snow where a pony had been shot and found enough frozen blood to make some broth.

Shackleton and his men reached McMurdo Sound seven weeks after they had begun their return trip. Their trek, accomplished mostly by hand-sledging, became known as one of the great feats of polar history. The expedition was a personal triumph for Ernest Shackleton, for he had pioneered nearly every step of the way.

In June, 1910, Robert Falcon Scott, then a captain, set sail once again for Antarctica. His previous expedition had been mainly in the interest of science; now he too was intent on reaching the South Pole. His confidence was dimmed considerably when he arrived in Melbourne, Australia, and found this telegraph message waiting for him: "BEG LEAVE TO INFORM YOU PROCEEDING ANTARCTICA. AMUNDSEN." It meant simply that Roald Amundsen, who had let the world believe he was heading for the Arctic, had

Dr. Wilson, artist for the Scott expeditions, drew this whimsical cartoon of an Antarctic sledge party. The robust-looking passenger on the sledge holds a banner whose Latin expression means "slowly."

103

Ernest Shackleton could not resist a challenge. He would never hesitate to risk his money or his neck on a venture he thought was worthwhile. Be it a cigarette factory in the United States or a gold mine in Hungary, he was quick to put down his money and direct all his efforts toward making good the gamble. The biggest gamble of his life, and the one he found most challenging, was his attempt to reach the South Pole. His confidence was such that he had little difficulty persuading a wealthy industrialist, William Beardmore, to finance a Shackleton expedition to Antarctica in 1908. The explorer is shown at left in full naval regalia and at right in a caricature by Wilson. Below is a photograph of the three men who went along with Shackleton on the journey that took them not quite to the South Pole—but only ninety-seven miles from it.

While Scott's supply depots were being laid, his ship, the Terra Nova *(in background), encountered Amundsen's* Fram *(foreground). Scott's ship had gone exploring in the Bay of Whales and found the* Fram *at anchor there.*

changed his plans. Admiral Peary had beaten him to the North Pole; now he was on his way to try to beat Scott to the South Pole.

In January, 1911, Scott arrived in the Antarctic and once again set up his base on McMurdo Sound. Like Shackleton, he hoped to rely mainly on shaggy Siberian ponies to transport him across the ice. He brought seventeen ponies with him, but nine of them were lost in various mishaps before the push to the Pole actually began. Scott also carried two motor vehicles and thirty-three dogs.

When Scott had sought the advice of Arctic explorers Nansen and Amundsen, they had urged him to use only dogs for sledging. But he could never accept the thought of killing and then eating the dogs when they wore out. However, he had absolutely no qualms about using the ponies in just this way. His disappointment with dogs, a result of his first expedition, became more pronounced now as he made mild attempts to master his half-wild sledge dogs. He could not bring himself to use a firm hand in dealing with them, and consequently he got almost no use out of animals that had proved their worth in the Arctic again and again.

By the time Scott's support parties had laid the supply depots, winter had fallen. With the return of spring, or what passes for springtime in Antarctica, the polar party set out. The men were forced to pull the sledges once they started up the Beardmore Glacier, because by then the Siberian ponies were all dead.

Scott's drive for the Pole was in many ways like Shackleton's. His men rose early each morning to a breakfast of tea and a kind of gruel called "hoosh." Then, after a day of dragging their sledges, they crawled wearily into wet sleeping bags at night. These were the common discomforts of polar exploration. But Scott, in his diary, commented on the strange weakness that had overcome him and his men. He blamed it on the cold and the difficult sledging, but it was probably the first sign of scurvy.·

The men ignored the warning symptom and pushed on, their strength buoyed somewhat by the thought of approaching victory. But eleven miles from the Pole their buoyant spirits collapsed, for they came upon a black flag, sledge and ski tracks, and the marks of many dogs in the snow. Apparently Amundsen had been there before them. Scott had been afraid this would happen, though he seldom mentioned it, ever since he had learned that the clever Norwegian was en route to Antarctica.

NORWEGIAN INFORMATION SERVICE, PHOTO BY WILSE

Roald Amundsen, who had failed to be first at the North Pole, was now racing Scott toward the South Pole.

Men of the Amundsen expedition plant the Norwegian flag at the South Pole on December 14, 1911.

"It is a terrible disappointment, and I am sorry for my loyal companions," he wrote that evening in the tent. "Many thoughts come and much discussion have we had. Tomorrow we must march on to the Pole and then hasten home with all the speed we can compass. All the daydreams must go; it will be a wearisome return."

The next day—January 17, 1912—Scott reached the South Pole. There he and his men found a tent flying the Norwegian flag, a sledge, and various other pieces of abandoned equipment. Inside the tent Scott found a letter addressed to him from Amundsen. It was dated December 14; Amundsen had reached the Pole more than a month earlier.

While Scott and his bedraggled party camped briefly at the Pole, trying vainly to predict their uncertain future, Amundsen was nearing his home base on the Ross Sea. His men were healthy, and his surviving sledge dogs were in excellent condition; some had even gained weight. There is perhaps no greater contrast in all polar history than the marches to the South Pole made by Scott and Amundsen, each within such a short time of the other.

To begin with, the Norwegians had established their base in an area known as the Bay of Whales. This was near the eastern end of the Ross Ice Shelf, opposite Scott's base

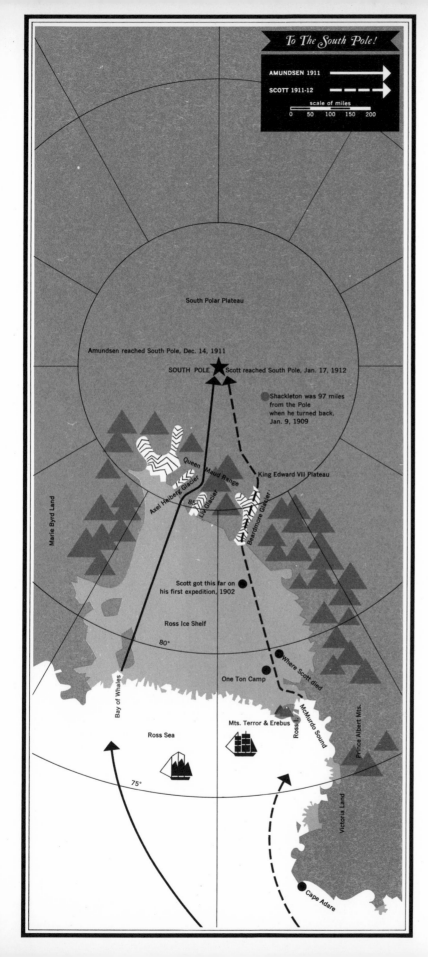

AMUNDSEN 1911

SCOTT 1911-12

scale of miles

0   50   100   150   200

South Polar Plateau

Amundsen reached South Pole, Dec. 14, 1911

SOUTH POLE   Scott reached South Pole, Jan. 17, 1912

Shackleton was 97 miles
from the Pole
when he turned back,
Jan. 9, 1909

Queen   Maud Range

King Edward VII Plateau

Axel Heiberg Glacier

85°

Liv Glacier

Beardmore Glacier

Marie Byrd Land

Scott got this far on
his first expedition, 1902

Ross Ice Shelf

80°

Where Scott died

One Ton Camp

Bay of Whales

Mts. Terror & Erebus

Ross Sea

McMurdo Sound

Prince Albert Mts.

75°

Victoria Land

Cape Adare

*The routes Amundsen and
Scott took to reach the South
Pole are seen on this map.*

109

Aug. 8.11 — &c Jara — Cape Evans. Looking North.

Amundsen used dog teams to sledge to the Pole; whereas, at first, Scott depended on ponies. In a blizzard like

this one painted by Wilson, the ponies were made miserable by the hard-driven snow that penetrated their coats.

on the western end. Five men, four sledges, and fifty-two dogs started the pole-ward dash on October 19, 1911, during the brief Antarctic spring. Once the long, arduous climb to the polar plateau had ended, it was no longer necessary to have so many dogs. So, in keeping with Amundsen's strategy of shooting superfluous animals, three dozen dogs were put to death. The dogs that remained, as well as the men themselves, ate some of the fresh meat before it was cached away for possible use on the way back.

The trip was so well planned and so efficiently carried out that it seemed less like an adventure and more like an organized tour. At 3 P.M. on December 14, Amundsen halted his men with a shout, and then he raised his arm. The South Pole had been reached without incident, and to

After reaching the Pole, Scott tried to sledge back to his ship at the base in McMurdo Sound. Above are seals resting on crusty "pancake" ice.

*On June 6, 1911, months before he left his Antarctic base to try to reach the Pole,
Scott sat down at the head of a long table (above) to celebrate his forty-third
birthday. Meanwhile, his wife (shown at top with their young son) prayed
for her husband's safe return. The pictures in the hut where Scott worked
on his diary (right) indicate that his family was always in his thoughts.*

115

judge by the explorer's own account, with little emotion:

"I cannot say—though I know it would sound much more effective—that the objective of my life was attained. That would be romancing rather too barefacedly. I had better be honest and admit straight out that I have never known any man to be placed in such a diametrically opposite position to the goal of his desires as I was at that moment. The regions around the North Pole—well, yes, the North Pole itself—had attracted me from childhood, and here I was at the South Pole. Can anything more topsy-turvy be imagined?"

The return from the Pole was accomplished easily. After the men reached the first depot, their food supply was plentiful. As Amundsen himself put it, "We had such masses of biscuits that we could positively throw them about." They reached their home base on January 25, having made the round trip in ninety-nine days.

At about this time Scott and his men were trudging painfully northward toward McMurdo Sound—a cluster of tiny figures silhouetted against an immensity of whiteness, accompanied by their constant companions, hunger, cold, and weariness. Their advance was dangerously slow, for the strange weakness Scott had noted in his diary made it increasingly difficult to haul the sledge. Progress was complicated further when Scott wrenched his back and Titus Oates, an army officer who was a member of the expedition, developed frostbitten feet.

Despite these afflictions, Scott remained as much a scientist as an explorer. At Beardmore Glacier he made side trips to collect fossils from rocks and coal seams. Thirty-five pounds of specimen material were packed on his sledge by the time he moved on.

As the men became weaker the task of pulling the sledge became tougher and tougher. "God help us," Scott wrote in his diary, "we can't keep pulling, that is certain. Amongst ourselves we are unendingly cheerful, but what every man feels in his heart I can only guess."

Soon Titus Oates' feet were so painfully frostbitten that he was literally dragging them, and he could no longer help pull the sledge. A man of pride, he loathed the

These photographs were developed from film that was found on the bodies of Scott and members of his expedition. At left above, the men bend their backs to drag a heavily loaded sledge to their destination. At left below is the sight that greeted Scott when he reached the South Pole—a tent, a flag, and evidence proving that Amundsen had been there first. Scott is seen at left.

thought that his slow progress had become a burden to the others. He begged to be left behind, but neither Scott nor the other two men would hear of it.

By the middle of March, Oates knew he could go no farther, nor could he allow his companions to pull him on the sledge. With his weight as a further drain on their waning strength they could not possibly survive. Early one morning Oates struggled to his feet. A blizzard was raging outside the tent, but he announced to the others, "I am just going outside and may be some time." He stumbled through the flap and was lost forever in the swirling whiteness.

Finding no trace of him, Scott and the others continued on without him. Their only hope for survival lay in reaching One Ton Camp, which was their largest and most important supply point. It promised safety because it had plentiful amounts of food and fuel. But the men of the expedition never reached this depot. Their progress slowed to a crawl, they made their last stop eleven miles from One Ton Camp on March 20. A blizzard set in and was still shrieking more than a week later when Scott grasped his pencil, and with numbed fingers, made this entry in his diary. It was dated March 29, 1912:

"Outside the door of the tent it remains a scene of whirling drift. I do not think we can hope for any better things now. We shall stick it out to the end, but we are getting weaker, of course, and the end cannot be far. It seems a pity, but I do not think I can write more.

R. SCOTT

For God's sake look after our people."

The next November a search party found the almost buried tent and the bodies of Scott and two of his men. The diaries and letters written during the men's last days were removed from the tent, but the men were allowed to remain as they lay. The tent supports were taken down, and the tent was lowered to cover the bodies. A cairn of snow blocks was built over them to mark the spot—until new layers of snow and ice would cover their resting place forever.

Dressed in attire that was probably as uncomfortable for them as it was unusual, three polar heroes are posed here like diplomats. From left to right: Shackleton, who came within ninety-seven miles of the South Pole, and Peary and Amundsen, who were first at the North and South Poles, respectively.

VII VOYAGE OF THE ENDURANCE

After the two poles had been reached, the great beckoning goals of Arctic and Antarctic exploration were gone. There was nothing more in these icy regions that could excite the world quite so much as the triumphs and failures of Peary, Amundsen, and Scott. By this time, too, the very nature of polar exploration was undergoing change. Machines and technical devices were becoming part of the explorer's equipment; the days when human courage and endurance were the chief defenses against blizzard and ice soon would be gone.

It was left to Ernest Shackleton to organize the last of the old-style polar explorations—man against the elements, with the odds opposing him. He was ever the gambler and the seeker of adventure, and at forty he was heartier and more persuasive than ever. His plan quickly caught the public fancy: to cross the Antarctic continent from one side to the other by way of the South Pole. The undertaking was adventure pure and simple, having no apparent scientific value—which is probably why it appealed so much to Shackleton.

On the surface, the plan seemed simple enough. A support expedition would land at McMurdo Sound on the Ross Sea and cross the Ross Ice Shelf, laying supply depots as far as the Beardmore Glacier. Meanwhile, Shackleton would approach the continent from its opposite side and land on the shore of the Weddell Sea. Then he would head for the Pole, and upon reaching it, travel the now-

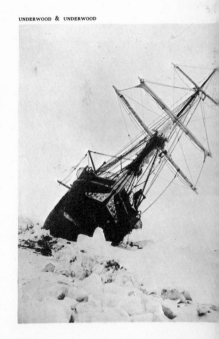

The abandonment of Shackleton's ship (above) and his attempt to reach South Georgia (left) marked the beginning and the end of one of polar history's most heroic chapters.

familiar route toward McMurdo Sound, tapping the supply depots during the last leg of the journey.

The plan, despite its simplicity, had built-in perils. For fully half of the journey Shackleton would have to travel over completely unknown territory. In addition, he would have to gamble that his support party would be successful in laying the depots and that he would be able to find them in the white, featureless desert.

Shackleton and his twenty-eight-man crew sailed on August 8, 1914, just four days after Great Britain had become involved in war with Germany. For the next four years the minds and hearts of nearly everyone would be caught up in the progress of the First World War. But, for much of this time, Shackleton and his men would be waging their own private war against the rigors of nature.

By the beginning of January, 1915, Shackleton's ship, the *Endurance*, was pushing easily through loose pack ice in the Weddell Sea, heading for a landfall in Vahsel Bay. But, less than three weeks later, the ship was hopelessly beset by the floes.

Pack ice in the Weddell Sea moves in a clockwise direction, due to the prevailing wind and water currents and the geography of the sea. The *Endurance*, caught up in the drift, moved farther and farther from her destination. The drift continued, with few incidents, until late the following July, when rumblings and grindings in the ice indicated the buildup of pressure. In its circling movement the pack was ramming itself, at its outer edges, against the rocky shores of Palmer Peninsula.

"The effects of the pressure around were awe-inspiring," Shackleton later wrote. "Mighty blocks of ice, gripped between meeting floes, rose slowly until they jumped like cherry stones squeezed between thumb and finger. The pressure of millions of tons of moving ice was crushing and smashing inexorably. If the ship was once gripped firmly, her fate would be sealed."

Soon, ice did grip the *Endurance*. She was thrown almost onto her side, and then a few hours later was dropped back on an even keel and squeezed as though she were in a monstrous vise. "It was a sickening sensation to feel the decks breaking up under one's feet, the great beams bending then snapping with a noise like heavy gunfire . . ." Shackleton declared. "The floes, with the force of millions of tons of moving ice behind them, were simply annihilating the ship."

The *Endurance* was abandoned. Men and dogs camped

on the floes, although the splintered, tortured wreck of the ship did not drop through the ice for a month after the men had left her. First plans were to drag the ship's boats on sledges to an island near Palmer Peninsula, more than three hundred miles away. Here, Shackleton recalled, food supplies from an earlier expedition were buried. The men spent several back-breaking days dragging the boats, but they gave up the attempt when they realized that they had advanced only a few miles. They made camp on the ice

Forsaken by her crew and crushed by the grip of the floes, the Endurance *is pulled slowly into a frozen grave in the Weddell Sea.*

The fate of the marooned voyagers depended on Shackleton's leadership. He is shown at right, next to a man who is stripping blubber from a seal carcass. When Shackleton ordered his men to leave the Endurance, supplies had to be unloaded and the dogs had to be weighed before the expedition could move. The men made camp on a large ice floe (below) for the next 165 days.

once again and then drifted, waiting until conditions would permit the boats to be launched.

Life on the floes was completely miserable throughout the long drift. Clothing quickly became saturated with the oily seal blubber used in making fires, and the men's faces were blackened by the greasy, clinging soot. Changing clothes was out of the question, and there was no way for the men to wash themselves.

Summer brought more discomfort—and greater perils. The men were constantly soaked and chilled by the melting snow. They waded through wet snow during the day and slept in snow-wet sleeping bags at night. Nor could they sleep peacefully, for the breakup of the pack ice frequently and unexpectedly caused the floes on which they rode to split open. Two or three times the widening channels cut through the camp itself, so it had to be moved.

Icebergs were an infrequent but more terrifying danger. At one point, two icebergs that had been advancing slowly toward the camp suddenly picked up speed, and as one man described them, "came charging toward us, plowing through the great masses of pack ice as though these had been tissue paper." When it appeared almost certain that the Shackleton party was doomed, the bergs, obeying a mysterious shift in ocean current, changed their course and moved away.

As the floes drifted northward, the ice breakup hastened. Soon the floe on which the men were camped had dwindled to the size of a raft. And the "raft" became smaller and smaller, until the men had no choice but to launch the three boats. It was March, 1916, more than a year since the *Endurance* had been beset and nearly six months since the men had taken to the ice. By this time they had drifted far to the north, beyond the tip of Palmer Peninsula. The nearest land was Elephant Island, about a hundred miles away. Shackleton directed the boats toward it. He had to reach the island; there could be no going back against the fiercely contrary wind and the sea currents.

The trip was made in utter misery. Gales lashed the tiny boats, and killer whales wallowed and spouted in the waters around them. Many men became violently seasick. And hands unaccustomed to rowing developed blisters and turned painfully raw. The approaching winter brought bitter cold accompanied by frozen clothing and frostbitten faces. One man's feet were so severely frozen that all of his toes were eventually amputated.

Elephant Island is a great chunk of rock whose towering

*Shackleton and five men set out from Elephant Island by boat (top), hoping
to get help for their shipmates who remain stoically on the beach (bottom).*

peaks and forbidding cliffs are barren and glacier-capped. The men of the *Endurance* sailed for hours along the craggy coast before they could find a scrap of beach on which they might camp. It was not a satisfactory place to stop, for the galelike winds roaring down from the cliffs ripped the tents to shreds almost at once.

Two boats were laid upside down over rock formations to provide shelter, and the presence of seals and penguins promised a reasonably steady supply of food. Shackleton decided quickly that he must try to find help before winter locked the island completely in ice. He had one boat decked over and strengthened as much as possible with lumber from the other boats. Then, with five men accompanying him, he set sail for the island of South Georgia, where an Antarctic whaling station was situated.

To reach South Georgia the men had to travel eight hundred miles on one of the world's stormiest seas. At times waves almost swamped the twenty-two-foot craft, and it seemed doubtful that the crew's frantic bailing would bring the boat up in time to survive the sea's next assault.

Soon ice began to form on the boat; it slowed down, threatening to founder. The men clung to the deck with numbed fingers and chipped at the slippery coating. Each one knew that if he fell overboard there was no way the boat could be brought about to pick him out of the water.

The boat finally landed on the rocky, wave-hammered shore of South Georgia, passing miraculously through a small break in the deadly, churning surf. Reaching the island was a superhuman feat, but it only partially solved the problem: the whaling station and South Georgia's few human inhabitants were on the opposite side.

Shackleton then made history's first crossing of the mountainous island; it was only twenty miles wide, but its peaks rose higher than seven thousand feet. He completed the perilous trek in thirty-six hours. Then, after four unsuccessful attempts to find assistance, he finally obtained a ship that could break through the ice-locked South Atlantic so he could rescue the rest of his crew.

The men of the *Endurance* returned to England in surprisingly good health. The only casualty had been the seaman who lost his toes from frostbite. Shackleton had not achieved what he had set out to do, but that he and his men had returned safely was a tribute to his courage, leadership, and extraordinary skill as a navigator. The voyage of the *Endurance* was a notable achievement, even though the great southern continent was still untraversed.

Awaiting rescue on Elephant Island, men of the Endurance *prepare for heavy storms. They are digging a shelter in the ice to cut the force of wind-blown snow.*

Richard E. Byrd (left) and his pilot, Floyd Bennett.

VIII POLE HOPPING IN THE AGE OF FLIGHT

The First World War had been over for a number of years before men began to think seriously of the polar regions again. By then, mechanization had altered completely the explorer's approach to investigating unknown territory.

The drama of polar exploration was not diminished by the new technology, but the introduction of new scientific methods and motives did signal the start of a new era of discovery. The old era's passing was marked, perhaps symbolically, by the death of Ernest Shackleton in 1922. Sailing in Antarctic waters to probe the coastal lands, the once indomitable Shackleton succumbed to complications that accompanied an attack of flu. He was buried on South Georgia.

Shackleton may have been the last of the old-style polar adventurers, but he was not the last polar hero. His Antarctic exploration was to be followed, some years later, by that of Richard E. Byrd, an American naval officer whose initial exploits took place in the North. Byrd's Arctic success had far-reaching consequences, for he added a new refinement to polar exploration.

On April 29, 1926, Lieutenant Commander Byrd arrived at Kings Bay in West Spitsbergen, leading his first polar expedition. Instead of sledges, dogs, and walrus blubber—typical baggage on expeditions of Peary's day —Byrd's ship, the *Chantier*, carried drums of oil, tins of

The return of Commander Byrd and Floyd Bennett from their historic flight over the North Pole in 1926 was painted (right) by Frank Wilbert Stokes.

En route to Spitsbergen, the ship carrying the plane in which Byrd would fly to the Pole became iced in. The plane was hauled to land on a raft made of the ship's boats.

gasoline, spare engine parts, and an airplane. The explorer planned to fly over the North Pole.

Getting a plane airborne in that early period of aviation was complicated by many primitive-seeming but very real difficulties. To thin the oil for lubrication, the big drums had to be heated over long-burning fires. To provide a flat runway for takeoffs and landings, the ice had to be chipped and pounded smooth. And taking off on skis proved to be a tricky operation. Three times Byrd's plane skidded into snowbanks and damaged its landing gear. When the supply of spare landing gear was gone, replacements had to be fashioned crudely from such items as boats' oars.

These hazards were at last overcome, and on May 9, when the weather had become favorable, Byrd and his pilot, Floyd Bennett, took off. They had some trouble navigating over the featureless white expanse of snow and ice, and a suspected oil leak gave them a scare. Otherwise the flight was not particularly dramatic. The plane reached the North Pole, circled it, and returned for a safe landing at Spitsbergen. Byrd had made the 1,440-mile round trip in about sixteen hours. Peary, in his dash to the Pole, had advanced only twenty-five miles a day even under the best conditions.

Among those on hand to witness Byrd's return was Roald Amundsen. The Norwegian explorer congratulated Byrd warmly, masking his own disappointment that once again his desire to make history at the North Pole had been thwarted. He was in Spitsbergen to await the arrival of the dirigible *Norge*, in which he had hoped to make the first flight over the Pole. Now Byrd had beaten him to it.

Amundsen's determination overcame his disappointment, however, and three days after Byrd's return he took off in the *Norge*. Amundsen's companions on the flight were Lincoln Ellsworth, an American, and Umberto Nobile, an Italian. They flew 3,400 miles from Spitsbergen to Alaska—a successful flight, but a perilous one as well.

As the *Norge* headed north ice began to coat its sides. Then, torn loose by the airstream from the whirling propellers, the ice was flung against the gasbags, nearly puncturing their thin skins. The weight of the encrusted ice made the airship difficult to maneuver, but the men were able to pilot it over the Pole, where they dropped American, Norwegian, and Italian flags. By this time the ice and the sub-zero temperatures had made many of the *Norge*'s navigation instruments useless. The airship's ultimate arrival in Alaska was plainly the result of courage and luck, not good planning.

Nobile and Amundsen later quarreled over the performance of the *Norge*, which had been built to the Italian's specifications. Nobile responded to Amundsen's criticism by persuading the Italian government to back him in another polar flight in 1928. His new airship, which was called the *Italia*, completed part of its mission and then crashed on the ice 180 miles northeast of Spitsbergen. A search was begun by many nations.

At first there was little hope that the expedition would be found, for there was no way to know where on the Arctic ice the dirigible had come down. Then an amateur wireless operator in Russia picked up a weak radio signal from the *Italia*. The signal's point of origin was determined, and planes and a Russian icebreaker converged on the scene to rescue Nobile and the other survivors.

Roald Amundsen had joined eagerly in the search, for it was his quarrel with Nobile that had prompted this enterprise. Piloting a French seaplane that had been placed at his disposal, he flew out across the ice to look for the missing airship. A float from the seaplane was found some time later, but Amundsen was never seen again. For him, the flight of the *Italia* had ended in tragedy.

While the search for Nobile commanded the attention of men of adventure in the North, Richard Byrd was planning an expedition to the South—one that was to make him the best-known Antarctic explorer of his generation. Byrd was directly responsible for focusing American national interest once again on the earth's southernmost continent.

In December, 1928, Byrd sailed through the Ross Sea to the Bay of Whales, the site of Amundsen's old base in Antarctica. Byrd led the most lavish expedition ever to

Amundsen (below) died on a search for Nobile, who was photographed (above), balanced like a tightrope walker, inside the dirigible Norge.

visit the south polar regions. His methods would have amazed Scott and Shackleton.

First of all, more than a dozen buildings were set up on the ice to form the base that Byrd named Little America. Then, hundreds of supply crates were piled in parallel rows and roofed over so that when buried by snow they would provide protected tunnels between the main buildings. Little America had electricity, telephones, and three tall radio towers to keep it in contact with the outside world.

The expedition made extensive geographical and geological discoveries and on November 29, 1929, set out to make history. Byrd, his pilot, and two companions took off on the first flight over the South Pole.

Byrd's course followed Liv Glacier, which provided a passage through the lofty Queen Maud Range. The headwinds in the mountains were so fierce that the plane was soon in danger of crashing into the ever-narrowing walls of the passage. The pilot tried to gain more altitude, but the plane had been made sluggish by a heavy load of emergency supplies and would go no higher. When its en-

The Norge, *a 348-foot dirigible which had been designed by Umberto Nobile, flew from Spitsbergen to Alaska by way of the North Pole.*

gines threatened to stall, the pilot shouted, "Overboard!"

Byrd and the others knew what to do. They tossed two 125-pound food sacks through a small trap door, and thus lightened, the plane climbed high enough to scale the peaks. Now there were no obstacles, only a vast white plain over which the aircraft flew to reach the Pole. "One gets there and that is all there is for telling," Byrd wrote. "It is the effort to get there that counts."

Four years later Byrd led a second expedition to Little America. Money was hard to come by then, so financial support could not be so lavish as it had been in 1928. But, compared with the standards of old-style explorations, this expedition was well equipped. Included among its effects were four airplanes and six motor vehicles—evidence of the increased mechanization of polar exploration. There were also 153 dogs; no one had yet found a substitute for dogs for trail work.

Despite the smooth organization of the enterprise, the perils were not eliminated. Part of Byrd's plan was to take winter weather-readings in the interior of Antarctica. This was an important project because the icy air that pours off the two-mile-high polar plateau has a marked effect on the earth's changing climate. A prefabricated cabin was dug into the ice about 125 miles south of Little America. Only its ventilators, weather instruments, and a trap door were above the surface, exposed to the shrieking blizzards. The cabin was 9 by 13 feet, too small for more than one person, so Byrd decided to keep the long, lonely watch by himself.

His quarters were cramped, so as often as possible—when the night was windless—he would take walks, thrusting bamboo stakes into the snow at intervals to guide him back to the cabin. One time, however, his attention lagged and he wandered beyond sight of his markers. Steeling himself against panic, he searched carefully through the darkness, moving in widening circles which he marked with snow blocks to avoid going farther astray. Finally, and luckily, he came upon one of the stakes and found his way back.

Another time, when he had to adjust a wind meter, he climbed out of the cabin at the peak of a blizzard. When he tried to go back below he found that the trap door had stuck and he was locked out. Death would have claimed him quickly as he stood unprotected in the storm. But by the purest good fortune he discovered a shovel that had been left outside and he was able to pry open the stubborn door.

At right, Richard Byrd climbs out of the snow-packed hut in which he nearly suffocated during a winter-long study of Antarctic weather in 1934. One of the ships on this expedition was an old icebreaker, the Bear, *pictured below.*

These trials were minute compared with a winter-long threat to his life, which he overcame stoically—an almost continuous exposure to carbon monoxide poisoning.

Only six weeks after his long vigil had begun, Byrd became sick. Nausea weakened him—and puzzled him too. What caused it? Why was he feeling ill? He realized finally that his oilstove was to blame. A leak in the chimney was letting deadly carbon monoxide fumes seep into the cabin. Although he tried, he was never able to repair the chimney completely; thus he remained on the verge of collapse for the rest of his stay in the weather station.

Byrd had to use the stove from time to time to keep from freezing, but he lit it as infrequently as possible, seldom cooking his food. When he made his radio reports to Little America, he was careful to conceal his state of health. He was afraid that a rescue would be attempted which, in the bitter cold of the Antarctic night, might result in a costly loss of lives. When a tractor train at last came to get him, he was so ill that the men who reached him had to wait two months until he recovered enough strength to make the trip back to Little America.

Byrd's third expedition left the United States in 1939, just as war was erupting in Europe. It was America's first official participation in an expedition to Antarctica since the disaster-bound ships of Charles Wilkes had sailed there a hundred years before. The government's revived interest was partly scientific but largely territorial. Other nations had already claimed most of the Antarctic continent, cutting it into triangular wedges like the slices of a giant pie. Only the slice between longitudes 80° west and 150° west was still unclaimed, and the United States was focusing attention on that tempting piece.

The government's position had always been that it would make no Antarctic claims and recognize none by other nations. Now the United States was proposing not only to send an expedition to the unclaimed section but also to set up permanent bases there. Byrd, now Admiral Byrd, called one of the new bases Little America III; it was about five or six miles from the Little Americas of his first two expeditions. Ice pressure and the weight of accumulated snow had pushed in the walls of the old buildings, so that the structures were now unusable.

Little America III was established to the west of the unclaimed section at a point that was easily accessible to ships and relatively close to the soon-to-be-explored portion of the Antarctic interior. The other base, called East Base, was set up near Palmer Peninsula, much of which had not yet been explored or mapped.

The expedition functioned smoothly and well, with little need for heroics. The men carried out the specialized jobs they came to perform—surveying the coastal mountains, examining the rocks of the mountain ranges, using seismic instruments to record earth tremors. There was even a party of men organized to search for new species of plant and animal life, as the Antarctic had yielded nothing to date but algae, mosses, and a few varieties of tiny insects.

New tools had made polar exploration more efficient; new methods were now making it less risky. Hardships still existed, however, but they were more easily overcome. Vitamin pills could prevent scurvy. Food parcels could be dropped from airplanes to men stranded in inaccessible areas. And if a man was wounded or became ill in camp, a radio message would bring a plane to the scene to fly him out right away, if necessary, or at least provide the man with first aid. The drama of polar exploration would never slacken—so long as there were questions to be answered, mysteries to be solved—but the age of polar heroes was beginning to fade.

Early in 1941 Little America and East Base were abandoned, and the Byrd expedition returned home. Within months, war absorbed all the energies and interests of the American people. Plans to have permanent bases in Antarctica were forgotten, as were hopes of laying claim to any parts of the southern continent. However, the great changes in polar exploration that had taken place between the two world wars would not be forgotten. And even greater changes were in store when a new and even more intensive period of exploration began.

Little America is framed by radio towers in this 1929 photograph taken during the long winter night. Byrd referred to this Antarctic base as the loneliest city in the world.

New York City gave Byrd a ticker-tape welcome after his first trip to Antarctica.

IX OVER AND UNDER THE POLAR ICE

When World War II ended, the Antarctic continent was as desolate as it had ever been. Only a few traces of abandoned bases were left to indicate that men had ever been there. The scattered debris of exploration and the graves of missing explorers had long since been lost in the white immensity, buried deep under ice and snow.

That situation was to change—radically and rapidly. In February, 1946, the first of the postwar explorers, members of a British scientific expedition, began to trickle southward. By the end of the year the trickle had become a flood: thirteen ships and 4,700 men of the United States Navy reached Antarctica, the largest expedition ever sent there.

The Navy had been eager to test its war-developed ships and equipment in polar waters, and this huge expedition—called Operation Highjump—was the result. The officer in charge of the project was the Antarctic veteran Admiral Richard E. Byrd. Before his death in 1957, Admiral Byrd was to lead still another expedition. It would be his seventh polar voyage and his fifth to Antarctica.

Operation Highjump accomplished more than just the successful testing of new equipment. In three months of intensive exploration it covered and photographed about 60 per cent of the Antarctic coastline, much of which had never been seen before. New mountains were also discovered, some of them fifteen to twenty thousand feet high.

After Operation Highjump, expedition followed expedition until the International Geophysical Year of 1957–58, during which the fever of Antarctic exploration reached its

The modern explorer's helicopter easily surmounts the glaciated ridges of Antarctica (left); his face mask (above) dulls the bite of the icy winds.

peak. Scientific observations were to be made in many parts of the world throughout the eighteen-month I.G.Y. period. But the greatest concentration of effort was aimed at Antarctica, about which least was known.

By the time the I.G.Y. began, fifty different bases had been set up in Antarctica, manned by scientists from twelve different nations. With concentrated purpose the scientists flew over the continent to study its geography. And they drove over its surface in sledges and motor vehicles, chipping at rocks, plumbing the depths of the ice, observing the southern lights, recording winds—engaging in the myriad activities required to learn about the land.

This was the newest kind of exploration, intended for specialists and technologists. But in the midst of it came an achievement that seemed almost out of place in the scientific earnestness of the I.G.Y. A British expedition set out to do exactly what Ernest Shackleton had once hoped to do: cross Antarctica, by way of the Pole, from the shores of the Weddell Sea to McMurdo Sound on the Ross Sea. The leader of this transcontinental passage was the English

Though it lends a bizarre note to this Arctic scene, the umbrella does have a function. It shields a light- and heat-sensitive theodolite, an instrument for measuring both horizontal and vertical angles.

polar explorer Sir Vivian Fuchs. Working with him was Sir Edmund Hillary, the man who had conquered Mount Everest. Hillary's purpose was to lead a support party to lay supply depots from McMurdo Sound toward the Pole.

The expedition had a number of purely scientific missions, one of which was to take regular weather observations. Another was to measure ice thickness by gravity readings and by seismic shots with under-ice explosions.

The Commonwealth Trans-Antarctic Expedition, as this British enterprise was called, put an advance party on the shore of the Weddell Sea almost two years before the actual crossing began. During the brief summer months preliminary explorations were made. A base named South Ice was established by airlift on the polar plateau. Finally a land trail was blazed between the sea and South Ice over four hundred miles of crevassed ice shelf. On November 24, 1957, the expedition at last got under way from Shackleton Base on the coast. Six vehicles with tanklike tracks supplied the power to transport it across the continent. Each vehicle pulled a train of sledges loaded with supplies.

Crevasses became troublesome almost at once. Sunken spots, indicating big openings in the snow below, appeared in the surface—even in places where the trail had been blazed only a month before. Men on foot preceded the machines over this dangerous stretch, probing the snow with aluminum poles or thumping with ice chisels for the hollow sound that told of dark emptiness below.

Finally, after twenty-nine days, the treacherous ice shelf was left behind and the explorers climbed onto the polar plateau. Two more vehicles were added when the expedition reached South Ice, and the sledges were loaded with everything needed for the long trip: tents, food, explosives, scientific equipment, and an extra supply of fuel.

The main party set out on Christmas Day, three days after dog teams had been sent ahead to mark trail. The danger of crevasses by now had passed, but progress was slowed because the surface had frozen into *sastrugi*. Machines and sledges were jostled and bounced over the rough, icy ridges; riding was downright painful.

On January 6 the vehicles caught up with the dog teams, and they traveled on together. On January 20, 930 miles from where it had started, the expedition reached the South Pole. Fuchs and his men were met by Hillary, who had finished laying the depots and had flown in from New Zealand's Scott Base on McMurdo Sound. Clasping hands, Fuchs and Hillary carefully shielded a rift that had occurred between them some time before their historic meeting.

Fuchs had fallen behind schedule because of bad weather and breakdowns of equipment. Hillary had cabled him advising him not to try to complete the entire transcontinental trek in one season. Annoyed, Fuchs had indicated that if necessary he would push on to McMurdo Sound without Hillary's assistance.

This difference of opinion was greatly magnified by worldwide publicity. Certainly it was no surprise to members of the expedition that Hillary, without rancor, was on hand to welcome Fuchs to the Pole. The two men met at the American south polar base, and after closeting themselves for five hours, settled their differences.

Hillary returned to Scott Base and then flew back to rejoin the Fuchs expedition when it reached the first supply depot. On February 9 Fuchs and Hillary set out together to complete the remaining five hundred overland miles to McMurdo Sound.

Despite the conveniences made possible by twentieth-century technology, the two men found that traveling across the frozen land-without-landmarks continued to present difficulties. The foremost problem was navigation,

The Trans-Antarctic Expedition, led by Dr. Vivian Fuchs, was an important part of Britain's participation in the 1957–58 I.G.Y. At left, Fuchs' dog teams and vehicles pause during their overland trek to the Pole. Above is a geological camp, one of the scientific adjuncts of the expedition. Below is the celebrated meeting of Fuchs and Sir Edmund Hillary at the South Pole.

143

Sir Hubert Wilkins' submarine Nautilus *was photographed (left) as it sailed from England in 1931 on an unsuccessful voyage to the North Pole. The crew posed on deck for the picture at center. At right is the American nuclear submarine* Skate *breaking through the Arctic ice. The* Skate *reached the Pole—and surfaced—in 1959, exactly fifty years after Peary sledged there.*

which was often made impossible by "whiteout," a condition in which snow and sky are so hazy and white that there is no apparent horizon to separate them. During one whiteout, Fuchs, who was driving his vehicle by compass, looked up in time to see three other vehicles coming toward him. They were part of his own expedition, as it happened; his compass, completely unreliable so near the Magnetic Pole, had turned him around in a complete circle.

The descent from the polar plateau was not made on the Beardmore Glacier, which Scott and Shackleton had used, but on Skelton Glacier, much nearer McMurdo Sound. The vehicles, with their sledges behind them, skidded from side to side on the steeper slopes as they inched their way down the slippery surface. The end of the long journey came none too soon, for the brief Antarctic summer was nearly over. During the descent from the glacier, blizzards had blown fiercely and the temperature had fallen to nearly 40 degrees below zero.

On March 2 Fuchs' four vehicles, decorated with flags and pennants, came within sight of Scott Base. Among those in the welcoming party were men from a nearby American base. They supplied a hastily assembled band that had much volume and good intentions, but little else. The English and New Zealanders found it difficult to recog-

nize their own national anthem, "God Save the Queen."

The Trans-Antarctic Expedition had covered 2,158 miles in ninety-nine days. As in most successful modern explorations, careful planning and efficient machinery had counted far more than human endurance. The new age of polar exploration was well under way.

Five months after this expedition had ended, the American nuclear submarine *Nautilus* set out to make history at the opposite end of the world. Cruising off the coast of Alaska, she slipped quietly below the surface and headed into the ice-covered sea to the North. She remained submerged for five days. When she came up again, near the northern coast of Greenland, the *Nautilus* and her crew had completed a feat of Arctic exploration as noteworthy as the Fuchs-Hillary expedition in Antarctica.

The *Nautilus* was not the first submarine to try to dive under the polar ice cap. Another sub—also named the *Nautilus*—had made a similar attempt twenty-seven years earlier. The Australian polar explorer Sir Hubert Wilkins had been in command of the ship, which was loaned to him by the United States. He had set out in August, 1931, and had given up less than a month later, returning to his starting base at Spitsbergen. Violent storms had plagued his voyage, and damaged diving gear had made it impossible for him to fulfill the purpose of the trip.

Despite his failure, Wilkins remained optimistic about the possibility of navigation under the ice and also about the commercial possibilities of a northern passage for cargo-carrying submarines. His theories were not to be substantiated until the nuclear-powered *Nautilus* achieved what he had set out to do.

On July 22, 1958, the *Nautilus* left Pearl Harbor, her course and her destination a secret—except to her skipper, Commander William R. Anderson. Anderson was faced with the problem of having to find at least three hundred feet of water before allowing his ship to dive under the pack ice.

He had good reason to be cautious. Pressure ridges of ice were known to extend far down into the water, and the *Nautilus* measured fifty feet from her keel to the top of her "sail." She needed plenty of headroom to pass safely under the ice. After searching with his echo-sounding gear, Anderson found the required ocean depth not far from Point Barrow and ordered the ship to be submerged. Soon she was passing under the pack at a comfortable depth, heading due north.

Now in a realm without sun or stars, the sub was piloted with the help of an array of complex instruments. The most intricate and remarkable of these was the inertial navigator. This device kept track of the vessel's course by

BLACK STAR, PHOTO BY EMIL SCHULTHESS

registering changes in direction and speed, much as a human being in a moving vehicle is able to observe and remember changes in speed and direction, even in the dark.

The men on the *Nautilus* lived and worked in a climate that differed immeasurably from that in which pioneer explorers had once struggled over the ice-choked Arctic Ocean. The temperature in the submarine was always 72 degrees, no matter how cold the water was outside, and an elaborate air-conditioning apparatus kept the humidity below 50 per cent. As for creature comforts, the food was excellent and the supply of jukebox records was plentiful; there was a library, a refrigerator for between-meal snacks, and two motion pictures were shown every day.

The voyage proceeded without incident. At eleven fifteen on the night of August 3, the submarine glided across—or through—the North Pole. Many men in many ships, from the time of Henry Hudson, had tried to sail across the top of the world; the *Nautilus* was the first one to succeed. On August 5 she surfaced at a point between Greenland and Spitsbergen and sent out messages by radio to report her achievement to the world.

The *Nautilus'* feat did not stand long as a singular accomplishment. Five days after she came out of the ice the nuclear submarine *Skate* went under it at almost the same place. The next year two other American nuclear subs dove under the ice and surfaced right at the North Pole.

Three Sno-cats, each pulling a sled full of supplies, set out over the white Antarctic plain. The lead "cat" is rigged with a device made of wooden beams and aluminum discs which is pushed ahead of the vehicle to detect crevasses.

What once had seemed impossible was now becoming commonplace.

The centuries of great polar exploration are past now; yet there is still much to be learned in areas that have already been explored. Many questions remain to be answered—about weather, glaciation, ocean currents, and sea life; and the mystery of what lies beneath the ice caps of Greenland and Antarctica has not been solved. But these questions require answers from scientists, not explorers.

In the Arctic little space remains blank on the map. Airplanes have flown over most of the Far North, land and

Polar exploration of the past and present is contrasted here as an American Globemaster *touches down on an icy runway behind a team of Antarctic sledge dogs.*

sea, again and again. It is no longer a region to be explored, but one to be developed. Mining engineers look for minerals and oil beneath its land surface today. And, as a front line of North American defense, it is laced with a network of radar warning stations. These are served by a small host of military men, technicians, and construction experts, all moving across areas that were once familiar only to Eskimos. Men live and airplanes land on sections of Greenland ice that were completely unknown fifty years ago.

Antarctica is more violent and inhospitable—and less well known—than the Arctic. Portions of it still have not been reached by men on the ground. But these areas cannot long remain untouched by ice-skimming helicopters and vehicles that travel easily over ice and snow.

At the end of the International Geophysical Year, a number of scientific bases in Antarctica were abandoned. But many remained, dotted across the great frozen wilderness; it is unlikely that the continent will ever again be deserted. Some of the bases have such unexpected comforts as shower baths, innerspring mattresses, electric blankets, and motion pictures. These are not the crude outposts of explorers preparing to move on to new adventures; they are the homes of men who plan to be around for a while and want to be comfortable.

Since the end of World War II, scientists and engineers have been at work to find new materials to build durable, lasting structures in the hazardous polar ice. They have begun building nuclear power plants to provide the light and heat needed to make living conditions bearable all year round, and some scientists talk seriously of constructing cities in the polar regions—huge settlements lying comfortably beneath transparent domes that let in light but keep out the cold. Thus the thought of setting up permanent polar colonies, where animals could be raised and foodstuffs grown, is far less remote now than was the hope of reaching the poles themselves a century ago.

As the world population continues to swell, crowding all the inhabited continents and islands, it becomes more of a certainty that future civilizations will populate the regions that are known today as polar wastelands. With the aid of science, men may succeed someday where the colonizing Vikings failed, thus proving that what was put on earth does indeed have a use for man. But, however these regions are used, and regardless of their ultimate value, the stories of the heroes who braved nature's harshest cruelties at the ends of the earth will never be forgotten.

The perils of the Arctic are suggested in this imaginative painting by George Baxter in which gallant men do battle with fearsome polar bears, and sailing ships cruise among grotesque icebergs that threaten to crush them. The seamen shown here are from a British navy expedition that helped look for the lost ships of Sir John Franklin.

AMERICAN HERITAGE
PUBLISHING CO., INC.

BOOK DIVISION

RICHARD M. KETCHUM, *Editor*

HORIZON CARAVEL BOOKS

RUSSELL BOURNE, *Editor*

MERVYN D. KAUFMAN, *Assistant Editor*

JUDITH HARKISON, *Chief Picture Researcher*

LUCY DAVIDSON, *Picture Researcher*

EVELYN H. REGISTER, *Picture Researcher*

ELAINE K. ANDREWS, *Copy Editor*

JANET CZARNETZKI, *Art Director*

GERTRUDIS FELIU, *European Bureau, Chief*

CLAIRE DE FORBIN, *European Bureau*

ACKNOWLEDGMENTS

The Editors are deeply indebted to the administrators of many private and public collections in which paintings, photographs, and articles of special value to this book were found. Foremost among them are Dr. G. De Q. Robin and staff, Scott Polar Research Institute, Cambridge, England; Mr. Patrick Drew, Royal Geographical Society, London; Mr. George H. Goodwin, Jr., Librarian at The American Museum of Natural History, New York City; Dr. James Mooney, Deputy Director of the Antarctic Projects Office, Washington, D.C.; and Colonel Louis J. de Milhau, Chairman of the Historical Committee, The Explorers Club, New York City. Special thanks are also owed to a number of persons whose knowledge of Arctic and Antarctic explorations led to the discovery of rare illustrative materials: Commander Richard E. Byrd, Jr., Mrs. Gunvor Bull-Teilman, Mrs. Marie Peary Stafford, Mr. Ralph A. Lenton, and Mr. Robert A. McCabe. In addition, the Editors wish to thank the following individuals and organizations for their assistance and for making available material in their collections:

Mr. Ernest F. Klages, Junior Warden, Kane Lodge No. 454, State of New York

Mr. Jon Embretsen, Manager, and Mr. Hans Aanestad, Assistant Manager, Norwegian Information Service, New York City

Mr. John L. Rawls, Division of Naval History, Smithsonian Institution, Washington, D.C.

Mrs. Agnes Brabrand, Curator of Prints, The Mariners Museum, Newport News, Va.

Mr. M. V. Brewington, Assistant Director, Peabody Museum, Salem, Mass.

Dr. Walter A. Wood, President, Mrs. Wilma Fairchild, Miss Nordis Felland, Miss Ruth Nabor, and Mrs. Dorothea Hanatschek, American Geographical Society, New York City

Mr. Holger Lundbergh, Assistant Manager, American Swedish News Exchange, New York City

Mrs. Maud Cole, First Assistant, Rare Book Division, New York Public Library

Mr. Wilson Duprey and Miss Elizabeth E. Roth, Print Room, New York Public Library

Miss Marie E. Roy, Assistant Secretary, and Mrs. Elizabeth Bauer, The Explorers Club, New York City

Rear Admiral Ernest M. Eller, U.S.N. (Ret.), Director of Naval History, Department of the Navy, Washington, D.C.

Mr. Frans Smekens, Curator, National Scheepwart Museum, Antwerp

Mr. Gerard Van Acker, Chief Librarian, Bibliotheek der Universiteit, Ghent

Mr. Tore Gjelsvik, Director, Nordisk Polarinstitute, Oslo

Special research and photography: New York—Geoffrey Clements, John Schiff; Washington, D.C.—Henry B. Beville; New Haven—Emiddio De Cusati; England—Timothy and Maureen Green—color photography, Zoltan Wegner

Maps designed by Charles Goslin

FURTHER REFERENCE

Readers interested in further examining the art and artifacts of the great age of polar exploration may find collections of varying kinds in many American cities. Three of the most important of these permanent exhibits are The Mariners Museum in Newport News, Va., The American Museum of Natural History and the American Geographical Society in New York City. Other exhibits that also are open to the public may be found in the following cities: Chicago—Chicago Natural History Museum; Dearborn, Mich.—The Henry Ford Museum and Greenfield Village; Hanover, N.H.—The Stefansson Collection, Dartmouth College; Montreal—The Arctic Institute of North America; Mystic, Conn.—Marine Historical Association, Inc.; New Bedford, Mass.—Whaling Museum and Old Dartmouth Historical Society; Salem, Mass.—Peabody Museum; San Francisco—Golden Gate Park (Amundsen's ship *Gjöa*); Sharon, Mass.—The Kendall Whaling Museum; Washington, D.C.—Smithsonian Institution, National Geographic Society, Combat Art Gallery; Winnipeg—The Hudson's Bay Company.

For those who wish to read more about polar exploration, the following books are recommended:

Anderson, Commander William R., and Blair, Clay, Jr. *Nautilus, 90 North.* Cleveland: World, 1959.

Andrée, S. A. *Andrée's Story.* Translated by Edward Adams-Ray. New York: Viking, 1960.

Barber, Noel. *The White Desert.* New York: Crowell Co., 1958.

Bixby, William. *The Race to the South Pole.* New York: Longmans, Green, 1961.

Byrd, Richard E. *Alone.* New York: G. P. Putnam's, 1938.

Byrd, Richard E. *Little America.* New York: G. P. Putnam's, 1930.

Caswell, John E. *Arctic Frontiers.* Norman: University of Oklahoma Press, 1956.

Debenham, Frank. *Antarctica, The Story of a Continent.* New York: Macmillan, 1961.

Fuchs, Sir Vivian, and Hillary, Sir Edmund. *Crossing of Antarctica.* Boston: Little, Brown, 1958.

Henry, Thomas R. *The White Continent.* New York: Sloane, 1950.

Kirwan, L. P. *A History of Polar Exploration.* New York: W. W. Norton, 1959.

Lansing, Albert. *Endurance.* New York: McGraw-Hill, 1959.

Mountevans, Admiral Lord. *The Antarctic Challenged.* New York: Grove, 1956.

Mowat, Farley. *Ordeal by Ice.* Boston: Little, Brown, 1961.

Nobile, Umberto. *My Polar Flights.* Translated by Frances Fleetwood. New York: G. P. Putnam's, 1961.

Schulthess, Emil. *Antarctica.* New York: Simon and Schuster, 1960.

Shackleton, Edward. *Nansen.* London: Witherby, 1959.

Stefansson, Evelyn. *Here Is the Far North.* New York: Scribner's, 1957.

Sullivan, Walter. *Quest for a Continent.* New York: McGraw-Hill, 1957.

INDEX

Bold face indicates pages on which maps or illustrations appear

153

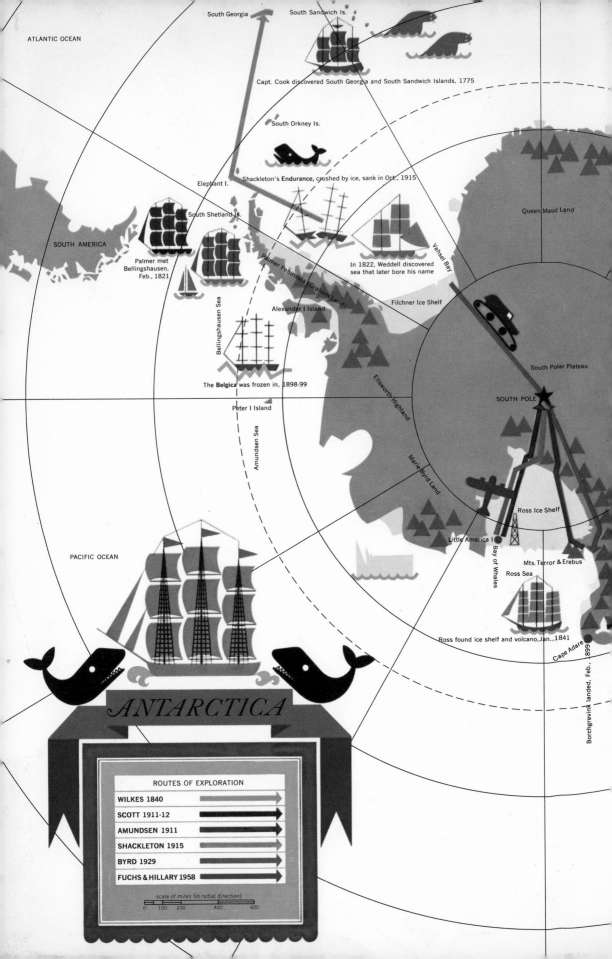

ATLANTIC OCEAN

South Georgia

South Sandwich Is.

Capt. Cook discovered South Georgia and South Sandwich Islands, 1775

South Orkney Is.

Queen Maud Land

Elephant I.

Shackleton's **Endurance**, crushed by ice, sank in Oct., 1915

South Shetland Is.

SOUTH AMERICA

Palmer met Bellingshausen, Feb., 1821

Palmer Peninsula (Graham Land)

Vahsel Bay

In 1822, Weddell discovered sea that later bore his name

Filchner Ice Shelf

Bellingshausen Sea

Alexander I Island

South Polar Plateau

SOUTH POLE

The **Belgica** was frozen in, 1898-99

Peter I Island

Ellsworth Highland

Amundsen Sea

Marie Byrd Land

PACIFIC OCEAN

Ross Ice Shelf

Little America I

Bay of Whales

Mts. Terror & Erebus

Ross Sea

Ross found ice shelf and volcano, Jan., 1841

Cape Adare

Borchgrevink landed, Feb., 1899

ANTARCTICA

ROUTES OF EXPLORATION

WILKES 1840

SCOTT 1911-12

AMUNDSEN 1911

SHACKLETON 1915

BYRD 1929

FUCHS & HILLARY 1958

scale of miles (in radial direction)

0   100   200   400   600